mini
Singapore

The Essential **Visitors'** Guide

Singapore mini Explorer
ISBN 13 – 978-976-8182-82-1
ISBN 10 – 976-8182-82-2

Copyright © Explorer Group Ltd 2007
All rights reserved.

All maps © Explorer Group Ltd 2007

Front cover photograph – Pete Maloney

Printed and bound by
Emirates Printing Press, Dubai, UAE

Explorer Publishing & Distribution
PO Box 34275, Zomorrodah Building,
Za'abeel Rd, Dubai , United Arab Emirates
Phone (+971 4) 335 3520 **Fax** (+971 4) 335 3529
Email info@explorerpublishing.com
Web www.explorerpublishing.com

Introduction

This mini marvel is the perfect companion for a stay on this fun-packed island – no matter how long. Written entirely by locals and long-term residents, the *Singapore Mini Explorer* is packed with everything a visitor needs to know, from Singapore's finest eating experiences to the best places to shop. If you want to know more about what we do, or would like to share your Singapore secrets, go to www.explorerpublishing.com.

The Explorer Team

Contents

Essentials

The Lion City

Welcome to a city of wondrous contrasts – a unique destination of ancient temples, modern malls, tropical parks and so much more...

Singapore is the ultimate city break, offering a taste of Asia in a clean, modern and safe environment. Whether you're in the city-state for just a few hours or can spend a week exploring, you're guaranteed to be seduced by the vibrant colours, world-class accommodation, delicious food and awe-inspiring views. Life here moves at a bit more of a 'tropical' pace than that of its neighbours Japan and China, but still offers plenty of buzz and excitement for visitors of all ages.

Singapore has a reputation for being a rather boring country with too many rules and too little fun. This is a huge misconception: you can do pretty much whatever you want in Singapore. Many of the strict rules that were in place 30 years ago have been relaxed as the city has been transformed from a sleepy village community to a bustling international business centre. As for the things you're not allowed to do – well, you probably shouldn't be doing them anyway. Common sense is the best thing you can take with you.

The mix of modern and traditional results in a huge variety of activities to keep you busy; from staggering malls to boat charters, you'll have no problems filling your days and the restaurants, clubs and bar scene mean the evenings will be action-packed too. But, if you're looking for a relaxing retreat then you've come to right place too. The huge

Singapore City

emphasis Singaporeans place on well-being means you'll find an amazing range of spas just waiting to pamper you into a state of bliss.

As with any bustling, fast-paced destination it can all seem a little daunting. In this mini marvel you'll find the to-dos, the must-dos and the don't dos, and as well as essential information for making your trip smooth sailing and fun-filled. We've provided a checklist of things you shouldn't miss starting on p.6, including eating in the hawker centres, hiking in tropical nature reserves and visiting the historic shophouses. You'll also find the best exploring (p.52) and going out (p.188) options organised by area so you can plan your day and get the most out your visit to Singapore. In fact, there's so much to do you might just need to come back.

Singapore Checklist

01 Raffles Hotel

The revered Raffles Hotel (p.74) remains a must-see. While an iconic Singapore Sling in the Long Bar (p.215) may not be to everyone's taste, roaming through the hotel complex is a pleasant way to enjoy its hushed, leafy courtyards and museum.

02 Hawker Centres

Forget the sanitised and air-conditioned foodcourts, the real eating action is still under a fan in an open-air hawker centre. Featuring anything from five to 50 separate stalls, with cool beer at decent prices, you can eat for as little as three dollars. See p.226.

03 Orchard Road

Big malls and bright lights, sometimes flashy and often tacky, the wide, tree-lined boulevard of Orchard Road is the place to suck in your cheeks, don sunglasses and designer shopping bags and play the age-old sport of 'see and be seen'. See p.170.

04 Sentosa

Singapore's 'leisure island' was first styled as a resort about 30 years ago and it's currently undergoing a bit of an upgrade. The new 'grown-up' entertainment of beach bars and destination spas will broaden its appeal. See p.110.

05 Singapore Zoo

Both Singapore Zoo (p.97) and the atmospheric, (world's first) night safari (p.96) are among the country's most innovative attractions. The magic is in the good condition of the animals, the lack of visible bars and carefully orchestrated feeding times.

06 Bukit Timah Nature Reserve

Singapore's nature reserves, located in the centre of the island, are popular escapes from the city, and the best is Bukit Timah (p.93). Hiking in virgin rainforest as monkeys leap overhead, it's easy to forget how densely populated this country is.

07 Riverside Meal

For early Singaporeans the centre of life was along the Singapore River. Now the area comes to life in the cool of the evenings with a good variety of cuisines and prices, and everything from loud rock music and sports bars to hushed, romantic, quayside dining. See p.244.

08 Chijmes

While it's not exactly conventional to dine and drink in a former convent, Chijmes somehow pulls its new incarnation off. Dotted with food and beverage venues, the wonderfully restored church offers a pleasant, quiet space. See p.71.

09 Shophouses

Whether morphed into bars, restaurants, brothels, or housing, the last protected tracts of shophouses are Singapore's most attractive heritage buildings. Duxton Hills, Emerald Hill (p.101) and Neil Road make for great exploring and photographing.

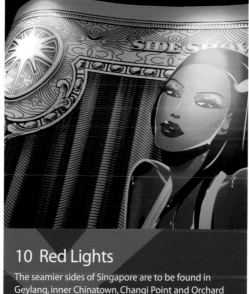

10 Red Lights

The seamier sides of Singapore are to be found in Geylang, inner Chinatown, Changi Point and Orchard Towers. They're worth exploring at night for their cheeky humour, cheap food and beer, and cultural insights you won't find elsewhere.

Best of Singapore

For Families…

As well as being one of the safest cities in the world, Singapore is very family oriented and children receive tremendous attention and pampering. With 20% of the resident population under the age of 15, this city-state is geared for children. Restaurants will normally have a children's menu and baby chairs. All the main malls (p.172) have good facilities for kids, as well as plenty of shopping options. Sentosa Island (p.106), East Coast Park (p.78), West Coast Park (p.121), Pasir Ris Park (p.80), and Singapore Zoo (p.97), are fabulous places for children, offering themed amusement parks and water parks and plenty of child-friendly activities. Many hotels will offer babysitting services, so check when you book.

For Budget Travellers…

With high quality hostels (p.48) popping up across the city, Singapore is no longer a destination exclusive to those with deep pockets. Eating out needn't break the bank either, with meals at Singapore's famous Hawker Centres (p.226), or the indoor version, Food Courts (p.226), costing just a few dollars for a range of quality, local cuisine. In the city, take a wander around the atmospheric areas of Chinatown (p.62) or Little India and Arab Street (p.84) for bustling examples of Singapore's ethnic origins. Further inland, in the centre of the island, visit the nature reserves to see some of the remaining virgin rain forest and enjoy hiking, canoeing or birdwatching. See Outdoor Activities on p.148. The many annual events and festivals (p.30) also give an insight into tradition, culture and the future of Singapore at no cost at all.

For Big Spenders…

If you've got cash to spend then you're in the right place. With upmarket hotels like Raffles (p.74) and The Fullerton (p.43), you can stay in the lap of luxury, while shopping at Singapore's finest malls on Orchard Road (p.170) will ensure you have no problem parting with your dollars. Purchases of note include electronics, camera equipment (p.185), or for a truly unique souvenir then a trip to the tailor (p.187) is in order. Singapore has an amazing eating out scene – check out the yellow stars in the Venue Directory in the Going Out chapter on p.194 for our recommendations. For cocktails before dinner, try bars like Bar Opiume (p.251) and New Asia Bar & Grill (p.218), then later finish up at Ministry of Sound (p.254) or Zouk (p.254).

For Short Stays…

If you're lucky enough to be stopping over in Singapore then you can get a real taste of the place in a relatively short space of time. Transit Tours (p.136) offer free two-hour tours from the airport; simply register at the visitor centre at Changi Airport. Seats are allocated on a first come first serve basis. If you've got a bit longer then head to Orchard Road (p.100) where you can enjoy food, drink, culture and shopping, all in one hot spot. With tiny boutiques, impressive malls and swanky restaurants, your whistle-stop visit can be action packed. Or to explore Singapore's history, (and its most famous hotels), head for the Colonial District (p.68). Combine this with a trip to Singapore Zoo (p.97) or the Singapore Night Safari (p.96), depending when you're in town, and you'll have big tales to tell from your short stay.

Visiting Singapore

Thanks to an award-winning airport and amazing efficiency, your arrival will set the tone for a memorable stay in this wonderful country.

Getting There

Year after year, Changi International Airport wins international awards for best airport in the world. The airport serves over 80 airlines flying from more than 180 cities in over 50 countries. Tourism is vital to the economy and the needs of travellers are met with exceptional efficiency. Even at peak times, it usually takes only 30 minutes to clear immigration, collect your baggage and clear customs. The city centre is 20 kilometres away (a 20 minute drive) but there's no need to hurry and many a reason to tarry.

Passengers can avail themselves of a massive range of amenities, from spa services, massages, a swimming pool, fitness centre, shower facilities, hotel accommodation, banks, ATMs, multi-faith prayer rooms, wireless internet...the list is long. Except for the specially designated smoking rooms, no smoking is allowed in the airport, not even in the taxi queue.

From the Airport

Transportation to and from the airport is easy. The most convenient option is taxi, which costs about $20 to the city. Alternatively, MaxiCabs can be shared by up to seven people, have flexible routing, and go to all major hotels and MRT stations downtown. Frequency varies from every 15 minutes (peak) to 30 minutes (off peak). Book at airport shuttle counters in the arrival halls in either terminal. Operating hours are 06:00 to 00:00. Adults cost $7, children $5, and cabs are wheelchair friendly. To the airport, the service runs from these pickup points: Concorde Hotel, Mandarin Hotel, Excelsior Hotel and Marina Mandarin, book with the hotel's concierge. Operating hours are 08:00 to 22:00.

For a bus, service 36 runs from Terminals 1 and 2 to Orchard Road. The fare is $1.70 and you should have the exact amount ready as no change is given. This is a normal bus service and stops en route to Marina Square and Orchard Road, looping back to the airport.

The MRT (Mass Rapid Transit) goes from Terminal 2 to Orchard station with stops at stations along the way. Fare is $1.70. The frequency of buses and the MRT is better than every 15 minutes. Generally, services operate from 05:30 to 00:00.

Visas

Visitors of many nationalities can get a visa (known as a social visit pass) upon arrival, for 30

Changi Airport

- **Terminal 1 covers can handle 21 million passengers a year.**
- **Terminal 2 can handle 23 million passengers.**
- **The airport can handle 18,000 bags per hour in departures and 10,000 per hour in arrivals.**
- **There are over 160 duty-free shops and 50 eateries.**
- **The Budget Terminal (www. btsingapore.com) was opened in 2006 for the growing number of budget airlines.**

days (if arriving by air) or 14 days if they enter overland from Malaysia. These countries include Australia, Canada, Japan, New Zealand, most EU countries, Norway, South Africa, Switzerland and the USA. Visas for other nationalities cannot be obtained at any immigration checkpoint in Singapore so application and approval must be processed prior to arrival. If you are in any doubt, check with an embassy or a travel agent for exact requirements before travelling, or visit the website of the Singapore Immigration & Checkpoints Authority (www.app.ica.gov.sg).

Beware; if you fly in and get a 30 day pass then later drive across to Malaysia, your 30 day pass becomes void the moment you cross the causeway. When you return to Singapore (via the causeway) you will only have a 14 day pass. Check the date that is stamped in your passport to be on the safe side, as one of the punishments open to the authorities for overstay of visas is caning (although it is unlikely for a simple, innocent overstay).

Duty-Free Allowances

Applies to persons over 18 years old and arriving from a country other than Malaysia.
- Spirits: 1 litre
- Wine or port: 1 litre
- Beer, stout or ale: 1 litre

There are no concessions on cigarettes and other tobacco products. Perfume is non-dutiable.

Customs

The government views customs offences very seriously. Customs officers will be polite and the whole process of clearing may appear cursory, but passengers are always observed. Some of Singapore's laws are very strict, and certain offences can result in corporal punishment or even the death penalty. Be particularly careful not to bring in any of the following prohibited items:

- Controlled drugs and psychotropic substances. (The sentence is the death penalty.)
- Liquors and cigarettes marked with the words 'Singapore duty not paid'.
- Chewing tobacco and imitation tobacco products
- Chewing gum
- Firecrackers
- Any imitation firearm including cigarette lighters in pistol or revolver shapes
- Endangered species of wildlife and their by-products
- Obscene articles and publications in any form
- Pirated goods of any type (software, DVDs and music CDs)

Medicines that require a prescription under Singapore law, for example, sleeping pills and stimulants, must be accompanied by a doctor's prescription.

Visitor Information

The Singapore Tourism Board (STB) is a great source of things to do and see in Singapore. Their main office is at 1, Orchard Spring Lane, just off Orchard Road (6736 6622). Additional locations include Liang Court Shopping Centre, Suntec City Mall, Singapore Cruise Centre on the HarbourFront and booths at Changi Airport in the arrivals halls at both terminals. They also have a 24 hour tourist hotline (1800 736 2000), and their website is rich with information: www.visitsingapore.com.

Local Knowledge

Climate

Singapore has an equatorial climate with little variation in temperature throughout the year, high humidity and plenty of rain. Average daily temperatures vary between highs of 31-32°C and lows of 23-24°C, although it can get as hot as 36°C and as cool as 19°C. The average humidity is 84%, though during heavy rain it can reach 100%. The average annual rainfall is 2,300mm. Due to a rain shadow effect, the east of the island is dryer and slightly hotter than the west.

There are two monsoon seasons. The north-east monsoon (December to early March), is known as the wet season, and brings strong winds and frequent heavy showers, mostly in the afternoon. The south-west monsoon (June to September) is milder, usually bringing scattered showers at midday. Maximum rainfall occurs in December and April while February and July are the driest months. Due to the high temperatures, raincoats are seldom worn but everyone keeps an umbrella or two handy (they're good for protecting you against the sun on hot, sunny days too).

Crime & Safety

In an international quality of life survey, Singapore ranked second after Luxembourg, and alongside Helsinki, Zurich, Geneva and Bern in the personal safety category. Its crime rate is also one of the lowest in the world. While 2005 saw an increase in the overall crime rate, it was mostly as a result of minor crime like theft from homes, or of mobile phones and bags. Travelling by public transport and taxis, however late at night, even if you are female and alone, is safe. While not commonplace, women in bars and nightclubs have had their drinks spiked, so don't leave them unattended.

Dos & Don'ts

There are plenty of don'ts in Singapore. Yes, you can get fined for spitting, littering or using abusive language. Smoking is banned in all government buildings, air-conditioned restaurants, shopping malls, sports complexes, and at taxi stands and bus stops. On the other hand you can walk down the street drinking a can of beer. Contrary to popular belief, chewing gum is not prohibited, but bringing it into the country or selling it is.

Do not 'jaywalk' (crossing a road within 50m of a pedestrian crossing or on anything but a perpendicular path to the pavement). Do not be rude to the police – they are accustomed to being treated with respect and they are expected to respect the public in return.

If you are contemplating consuming illegal drugs, you must be mad! Singapore has an absolutely zero tolerance policy – you will not get away with a warning, even if you are a tourist. The courts have set a sentencing policy of at least six months to a year in prison for first time drug users; recent cases indicate there are no mitigating

Chinese Names

The family name comes first followed by the given name, usually made up of two characters. Thus prime minister Lee Hsien Loong's surname is Lee. If you are on first name basis, you would call him Hsien Loong. If you are a close buddy (or terribly rude) you might call him Loong for short.

factors. There is also legislation to convict someone who fails a drug test in Singapore even if they consumed the drugs in another country. Minors are sometimes prosecuted as adults for drug offences. In addition, if you are found to be illegally importing controlled drugs such as heroin, marijuana or morphine into Singapore, the offence is punishable by death.

Electricity & Water

The electricity supply is very reliable and comes in 220/240 volts, 50Hz mostly using a square three pin plug, the same as the British system, as well as some two pin plugs on smaller applicances. Many hotels will loan you a suitable adaptor or transformer for appliances with a different voltage. Tap water is very safe and most residents drink it. Bottled water is commonly available in shops and restaurants.

Language

Singapore has four official languages : Malay, Chinese (Mandarin), English and Tamil. Malay is the national language but English is the unifying language between all the various ethnic groups – only the elderly may not understand any English. Road signs and all signage are in English, while official public notices are either in English and Chinese or in all four official languages. With over three quarters of the population speaking Mandarin as their mother tongue, it's always appreciated if you make the effort to communicate in the local language. See the Mandarin for Beginners table opposite.

Something that confuses some visitors is Singlish, a colloquial pidgin-like form of English widely used by

Singaporeans. It is a combination of Chinese grammar literally translated into English, and uses Chinese and Malay words. For instance: 'Why you so like that?' (grammatically perfect if spoken in Mandarin). Most Singaporeans either can or do speak Singlish, but as everyone speaks English extremely well, they aren't likely to use it often when talking to tourists. For more on this slice of local colour, see www.talkingcock.com and click on dictionary.

Lost & Found

All public transport and taxi companies have a lost property department and taxi fare receipts include the taxi number for reference. For enquiries about lost and found items on the MRT (metro), call 1800 336 8900. For a suspected theft, file a report at a police station. Don't call 999 unless it's an emergency or for a serious crime. For lost or stolen passports, you should make a police report immediately, then go to your embassy or high commission to obtain the necessary travel documents.

Mandarin for Beginners

Yes	shì [shir]	Toilet	cè suǒ [cher swore]
No	bú [boo]	Hello	nǐ hǎo [nee how]
Correct	duì [dway]	How are you?	nǐ hǎo [nee how]
Wrong	bú duì [boo dway]	Fine	hěn hǎo [hern how]
Please	qǐng [cheeng]	Good morning	zǎo ān [chao arn]
Sorry	duì bù qǐ [dway boo chee]	Good afternoon	wǔ ān [woo arn]
Thank you	xiè xiè [sieh sieh]	Good night	wǎn ān [warn arn]
You are welcome	bú kè qì [bu ker chee]	Goodbye	zài jiàn [chai chian]
Good	hǎo [how]		

To avoid a great deal of hassle if your personal documents go missing, make sure you keep one photocopy with friends or family back home and one copy in a secure place, such as your hotel room safe, along with a note of any IDs you might need and telephone numbers for cancelling credit cards.

Money

While cash is still the preferred mode of payment, the use of credit cards is extensive and commonplace – even taxis accept them. Apart from hotels, which accept some of the major foreign currencies, all other transactions should be in Singapore's currency. Most shops, department stores, supermarkets and restaurants do not accept cheques.

The local currency is the Singapore dollar, which is usually referred to by just the dollar sign, or by S$ or SG$. Its full international currency code is SGD. Notes come in denominations of $1, $2, $5, $10, $50, $100, $500, $1000 and $10,000, with coins in 1 cent, 10 cent, 20 cent, 50 cent and $1 denominations. New polymer $2 and $10 notes are now in circulation and the $1 coin is replacing the $1 note.

An extensive network of ATMs is spread across the island. ATMs accept AMEX, Cirrus, Mastercard, Overseas' Plus, Visa and Visa Electron, although the precise service provided depends on the bank's ATM – look for the logos on the machine.

Singapore has numerous money exchanges, known locally as money changers. They must be licenced and operate from a registered location. Tiny booths can be found in most malls and shopping complexes. Exchange rates at a money changer are invariably better than at a bank or hotel, and they handle a wider range of currencies. Do not change money with someone who walks up to you on the street – it'll be a con.

A lot of smaller shops and stalls won't take credit cards, and some places have a minimum purchase amount for payment by card, usually $20. Almost all restaurants and cafes take credit cards, but food courts and hawker centres don't. At pubs or nightclubs it's common practice to leave a running tab, where your card is held by the cashier until you leave. This practice is generally safe, but can leave you vulnerable to 'card skimming', so check your bill carefully. A 10% service charge is automatically included in all bills.

Sir Stamford Statue

People with Disabilities

Although progress has been made with regard to facilities for the physically challenged, there's still considerable room for improvement. Changi Airport is ahead of the game in these matters and no problems should be encountered there. The MaxiCab airport shuttle service (6456 4222) offers proper wheelchair facilities while Citycab Taxis (6552 2222) also cater for wheelchair users. Elsewhere, all car parks have some spaces reserved, most major buildings have special toilet facilities and newly renovated food courts come with wheelchair friendly tables. Only a few hotels have specially adapted facilities, so it's best to check before you book.

Public Toilets & Amenities

Singapore has more than 750 public toilets and with the extensive malls offering excellent facilities it's unlikely you'll be caught short during your stay. The 2003 campaign 'Singapore's OK' has ensured all public toilets provide a cleaner during peak hours so standards across the city-state are good.

Telephone & Internet

Public phones use either coins or phone cards, which are available at all post offices and many convenience shops. Overseas calls can be made from these phones. Dial 001 for IDD access. Pre-paid phone cards are easily available. Outlets such as McDonald's and Starbucks provide wireless broadband access – some for free. Virtually all hotels offer internet access and internet cafes are easy to find.

Time

Singapore is eight hours ahead of Universal Coordinated Time (UCT), formerly known as GMT. The clocks remain constant throughout the year as no adjustments are made for daylight saving. Sunday is the official day off for everyone but many commercial outlets remain open. Retail outlets, in particular the large department stores and supermarkets, usually open at 10:00 and close at 21:30. Restaurants tend to close by 23:00 and bars between 24:00 and 04:00. There is no lack of shops serving food 24 hours a day.

Tipping

While it isn't generally expected, tipping is definitely welcomed by recipients. Although not required to tip taxi drivers, tour guides and hotel staff, it's customary to tip valets and porters a dollar or so. When dining out, a 10% service charge is usually included on the bill in place of tips. Ask for it to be removed if the service was horrendous. Tips do not go to specific waiters so if you wish to thank a particular waiter, give them cash and let them know the tip is personally for them.

Postal Services

Singapore's postal service, SingPost (www.singpost.com), is efficient and reliable. Branches are spread across the island, and post boxes can be found at shopping centres, on most commercial roads, and often at petrol stations. Rates for a 20gm letter for international mail ranges between $0.60-$1.00, and it takes 7-12 days to reach almost anywhere.

Public Holidays & Annual Events

With such a diverse population there is always something going on and if you time your visit well, you could see an unexpected side to Singapore.

There are 10 public holidays a year, celebrating key religious events or new year festivals on the Chinese, Muslim, Hindu, Buddhist and Christian calendars, as well as Labour Day and National Day. Chinese New Year, Hari Raya Puasa, Hari Raya Haji, Vesak Day and Easter follow the lunar calendar and change accordingly each year. Nevertheless, these dates are fixed many months in advance.

Hari Raya Haji (Feast of the Sacrifice) is the new year for Muslims who follow a lunar calendar. Hari Raya Puasa marks the end of Ramadan, a month of fasting and purification. Vesak Day commemorates the birth, enlightenment and death of Buddha. Deepavali is celebrated by Hindus and symbolises the victory of good over evil.

If a public holiday falls on a Sunday the following Monday becomes a holiday.

Public Holidays (2007)	
1 Jan	New Year's Day
18 Feb	Chinese New Year
6 Apr	Good Friday
1 May	Labour Day
31 May	Vesak Day
9 Aug	National Day
13 Oct	Hari Raya Puasa (Aidilfitri)
8 Nov	Deepavali (Diwali)
20 Dec	Hari Raya Haji
25 Dec	Christmas Day

ARTSingapore

October
Suntec City

www.artsingapore.net

Over 50 leading art galleries gather to network and showcase the works of more than 400 contemporary Asian artists from the region. Corporate and individual buyers welcome.

Children First!

March

www.childrenfirst.com.sg

The Singapore International Festival for Children presents high quality performing arts experiences to inspire, nurture and showcase children's arts.

Navaratri

October

www.heb.gov.sg

Navaratri, meaning 'nine lights' in Tamil, celebrates three Hindu goddesses in different temples with song, dance and prayers for three nights each. Visitors are welcome to join in.

Singapore Arts Festival

June

www.singaporeartsfest.com

This major festival is truly international and features world premieres. The core programme has over 75 performances of dance, theatre and music from around the world.

Singapore International Film Festival

April

www.filmfest.org.sg

A film festival offering over 300 films from 45 countries showcasing Asian and world cinema, with an emphasis on regional documentaries and Singaporean short films.

Singapore Open

November

www.singaporeopen.org
Sentosa Golf Club

With a purse of US$2 million, this is by far the richest golf event in Singapore. The tournament will bring together the cream of Asian golfers and a select group of star players from overseas.

Thaipusam

February

A colourful, spectacular Hindu festival where devotees carry a beautifully decorated kavadi (yoke of burden) weighing 20-60 kilograms for about 5km along Serangoon Road to Thendayuthapani Temple. Parts of the devotees' bodies are pierced with metal spikes which makes for some interesting viewing.

WOMAD

August

www.womadsingapore.com
Fort Canning Park

Held over three evenings in August each year, WOMAD is a festival showcasing the award-winning artists from the travelling World Of Music And Dance festival each year artistes. Set in a beautiful outdoor venue at Fort Canning Park, it's the perfect setting for a picnic

World Book Fair

May

www.bookfair.com.sg
Suntec City

The largest and best known book fair in the region, it is the ultimate browsing and book experience for the 700,000 book lovers that come. to see the latest publications and electronic book products.

Sri Mariamman Temple

Media & Further Reading

A little online research and wider reading will help you get the most from your visit, and keep an eye out for listings magazines once you arrive.

Newspapers & Magazines

Singapore has seven major daily newspapers, with four in English. *The Straits Times* is the main English language daily. *The Business Times*, *The New Paper* (an afternoon tabloid) and *Today* (circulated free), are also in English. The free magazine *IS* will keep you up-to-date with what's happening in town, and is available in many pubs, restaurants and at information centres.

Television

Singapore has a reasonable selection of local TV channels but only two of them are in English. Channel 5 consists mainly of western programming with an emphasis on the latest dramas, comedies and reality shows from the US. ChannelNewsAsia (CNA) is a local version of CNN found on channel 32. Channel 8 shows many local dramas in Mandarin with English subtitles.

Radio

There are numerous radio stations broadcasting in English, in Singapore. Perfect Ten on 98.7FM provides contemporary hits while the BBC World Service is broadcast in English on 88.9FM. The International Channel at 96.3FM airs programming in Japanese, German and French.

Books & Maps

In Singapore, most bookshops and hotels carry eating out, entertainment and shopping guides. There are a good number of independant publishers producing guides, photography books and a variety of other publications on all aspects of Singapore. The 'bible' of Singapore's foodies, *Makansutra,* is a guide to 1,000 of the best eating places, typically hawker stalls and mid-range restaurants, by an acknowledged food guru. For more information on Singapore's shopping scene, pick up a copy of *Shopsmart Singapore* or if you are looking for a detailed street atlas, try *Street Atlas Singapore* from Periplus.

Websites

There are a whole host of websites packed with info on Singapore. For some of the best, see the table below. Another source of online info are blogs, such as Mr Brown (www.mrbrown.com), Miss Izzy (www.missizzy.org) and Only Slightly Pretentious Food (www.epicurative.blogspot.com), which give a fun, personal insight into life in the city.

Media & Further Reading

Websites	Information
www.visitsingapore.com	Singapore Tourism Board website
www.sg	Comprehensive portal of links and info
www.hotels.online.com.sg	Singapore hotels
www.nparks.gov.sg	Public parks
www.smrt.com.sg	MRT and bus guide
www.streetdirectory.com	Detailed street maps
www.sentosa.com.sg	Sentosa Island

Getting Around

With a wide variety of efficient and high quality public transport, travelling around Singapore is a comfortable and cheap experience.

Singapore is possibly the most expensive place in the world to own a car, a situation created by the government to ease traffic jams and the car population. This has resulted in an outstanding public transport system, which is cheap, comfortable, really convenient, and used by tourists and residents alike. The city is also very pedestrian friendly, with most roads providing footpaths, but the weather makes walking a rare luxury. If you are travelling any distance, it's much better to use a combination of the MRT (Mass Rapid Transit), bus network and taxis.

Boat

To get to the southern isles of Kusu, St. John's, Lazarus and the Sister Islands (see Outer Islands on p.124), use the Sentosa Ferry Terminal at Clifford Pier (Map p.296 C2); regular trips run daily. Ferries to Pulau Ubin (p.124), a popular island just 10 minutes north east of the main island and 40 years back in time, operate from Changi Point Ferry Terminal (Map p.277 F2).

Bus

As buses are one of the primary modes of public transport in Singapore, the level of service is high and it's impressive by

world standards. Dedicated bus lanes ensure timely arrival even during peak hour traffic jams. Depending on the bus route and time of day, service frequency ranges from 8 to 30 minutes. Buses provide seats and standing room but the number of passengers allowed to stand is strictly monitored.

Seats are usually available, but if a bus is full, even in peak hours, you'll not have to wait long for another one. Exact fares are required as no change is given. For convenience use an ez-link card (www.ezlink.com.sg), where a discounted fare will be deducted. It also works for the MRT. Buy one, or top it up, at any bus terminal or MRT station where bus guides are also available. Normal services operate 05:30 to 23:45 and the maximum fare is $1.90.

Car

Car ownership is extremely low amongst residents of Singapore, due mainly to the high costs involved. However, if you do get behind the wheel, roads are excellent and suited to wet weather conditions, expect local drivers to be law-abiding, generally thoughtful, but not always very courteous.

Vehicles are right-hand drive and traffic drives on the left-hand side of the road. Unless otherwise stated, the speed limit is 50kmh on roads and 70-90kmh on expressways. Cameras at traffic lights, speed detectors and traffic police patrols work to keep motorists in check.

There are many car rental companies (see the table opposite), from large well-known international names to small local companies. Between them you can choose from 1.3 litre budget sedans, SUVs, Mercedes and BMWs to exotic sports cars. For a standard 1.6 litre saloon car, average prices range from $70-150 per day. Check the Damage Excess payable in the event of an accident and consider buying a Collision Damage Waiver, which can reduce the payable amount from, for example, $2,000 to $300. Most rental companies restrict driving to within Singapore only. If you're in Singapore for less than a year, all you need is a valid foreign driver's licence.

The legal alcohol content limit is 80mg per 100ml of blood. If alcohol is detected and under the legal limit, the driver can still be convicted if they did not have proper control of the car.

Car Rental Companies

ATS Rent-a-Car	6732 0304	www.atsrentacar.com
Avis	6737 1668	www.avis.com.sg
C&P Rent-A-Car	6736 6666	www.candp.com
CityLimo	6882 0882	www.citylimo.com.sg
DownTown Travel Services	6334 1700	www.dts.com.sg
Expat Motors	6722 8420	www.expatmotorsingapore.com
Falcon-Air	6452 0880	www.falconair.com.sg
Hertz Rent A Car	1800 734 4646	www.hertz.com
Motorway	6468 2200	www.motorway.com.sg
ORIX Car Rentals	6319 8000	www.orix.com.sg
Popular Rent A Car	6742 8888	www.popularcar.com
Premier Rent A Car	6732 3375	www.premier-rentacar.com
Samly Limousine	6746 2692	www.samlylimousine.com.sg
San's Car Rentals	6734 9922	www.sanstours.com
Siang Hock	6256 8888	www.sianghock.com.sg
Smart Car Rental	6485 7788	www.smartcarrental.com.sg

Parking is rarely a problem but with a few exceptions, you'll have to pay for it. The exceptions are side streets in residential areas, on Sundays and public holidays in some car parks, and after 17:00 on some roads. All shopping centres, commercial buildings, hotels and some public car parks have a paid parking system where you pay for the time parked. Charges vary and can cost $2 per half hour. A variety of payment systems are used: a parking attendant, ticket, IU or CashCard.

Cycling

Not a recommended way to get around – it's either hot (average 32°C), humid (84%) or it's raining. However, cycling does have a following among avid enthusiasts. Outlying areas like Sembawang Road, Changi Coast Road and East Coast Parkway offer nice roads where cycling can be pleasurable. For mountain biking, there are some great trails at Bukit Timah Nature Reserve (p.93) and on Pulau Ubin Island (p.124).

MRT (Metro)

The MRT (Mass Rapid Transit) is Singapore's equivalent to the London Underground or New York's subway. It's an excellent way to get around: modern, air-conditioned, fast and inexpensive ($0.80-$1.70). Operating hours are from 05:30-00:30 (but vary slightly between stations), and while it can get crowded, train frequencies are adjusted to cope with this.

Single trip tickets valid for a day can be purchased from vending machines in every station. A $1 deposit for the smart card is automatically deducted and refunded via the vending machines. Remember to collect your deposit when you reach your destination. Three main lines span the island, and feeder services by the bus network and LRT system (Light Rail Transport) make it even easier to get to an MRT station. For frequent use, buy an ezLink fare card from a station ($15) which works seamlessly between the three transport systems. For more about the MRT, visit www.smrt.com.sg.

Taxi

An excellent way to get around Singapore, taxis operate 24 hours a day, are reasonably priced, well regulated and efficient. They have computerised booking systems and you can pay by credit card. Tipping is not normally required. Catching one is easy – just flag one down or go to one of the taxi stands located outside most malls and hotels. Fares and surcharges do vary but expect a flag down fare of about $2.40 including the first kilometre, increasing at about $0.50 per kilometre. A 50% midnight surcharge applies until 06:00. The fare automatically includes surcharges such as travel from the airport and toll charges. Drivers' road knowledge varies considerably; it's best to have some idea of a landmark near your destination and to speak clearly.

Walking

Frequent rain, average daytime temperatures of around 32°C and a mean relative humidity of 84% can make walking uncomfortable. That said, Singapore is very pedestrian friendly, particularly around tourist areas. It's against the law to jaywalk so use bridges and crossings, or cross at traffic lights. Don't assume cars will stop at pedestrian crossings.

Places to Stay

From exquisite hotels complete with grand decor and exemplary service to the cheap and cheerful backpacker hostel, the choice is yours...

Singapore has about 225 registered hotels, from one to five-star, and competition is intense. The hotel industry is well monitored by the Hotel Association and Singapore Tourism Board. Most of the five and four-star hotels are concentrated in the prime Orchard Road area and around Raffles City and the CBD. There are only three hotels with beach access, Shangri-La's Rasa Sentosa Resort (p.47), The Sentosa Resort and Spa (p.45), both on Sentosa Island, and a resort on the wilder island of Pulau Ubin, Marina Country Club Ubin Resort (p.126).

The average room rate in Singapore is around $120 per night, relatively cheap compared to North America and Europe, yet service standards are as high, or higher.

In the last few years, several boutique hotels have opened, offering cosy, luxurious accommodation in old, converted shophouses with personality as a primary selling point, underpinned by high services standards and modest prices.

Backpackers, once sneered at by mainstream hoteliers are now welcomed. Numerous hostels have sprung up to cater to this market (see p.48). The serviced apartment sector is also growing as new companies enter the market and as established ones expand. Some hotels are converting some of their existing rooms into serviced apartments.

Changi Village Hotel
www.changivillage.com.sg
6379 7111
With its chic interior and impressive landscaped gardens, this hotel is far from the city, but close to Changi beach and is good for leisure and business. Rooms are modern, with all amenities, and there's a rooftop pool.

Somerset, Map p.277 F2

Conrad Centennial
www.conradhotels1.hilton.com
6334 8888
Superlative luxury marks this award-winning hotel. The ambience is a stylish combination of Asian influences and contemporary chic. The fitness centre is open 24 hours and the pool offers panoramic views of the city.

City Hall, Map p.291 E3 **1**

The Fullerton Singapore
www.fullertonhotel.com
6733 8388
Located on the river, this neo-classical building was built in 1928. Transformed into a deluxe hotel, the Fullerton is considered to be a six-star property, offering old world charm with ultra-modern amenities.

Raffles Place, Map p.296 C1 **2**

Goodwood Park Hotel
www.goodwoodparkhotel.com
6737 7411
This Preferred Heritage Hotel was built
in 1900 in classical European style, and
is a historic Singapore landmark and a
designated national monument. There are
two pools, a fitness centre and spa facilities.
🚇 Orchard, Map p.282 C2 **3**

Orchard Hotel
www.orchardhotel.com.sg
6734 7766
This medium size hotel is cosmopolitan in
design, and is well situated on the popular
Orchard Road. It has an excellent Cantonese
restaurant, Hua Ting (p.231), and at the
poolside you can enjoy snacks and cocktails.
🚇 Orchard, Map p.282 A2 **4**

Raffles Hotel
www.raffleshotel.com
6337 1886
Established in 1887, the Raffles Hotel is the
crown jewel in Singapore's hotel industry.
Originally a sprawling colonial bungalow, it
has retained the inimitable style of that era.
For more on the hotel, see p.76.
🚇 City Hall, Map p.291 D2 **5**

Raffles the Plaza

www.singapore-plaza.raffles.com

6339 7777

This hotel has long been associated with sophistication and elegance and is situated close to culture, entertainment and shopping. There are 17 distinctive restaurants and bars, and Amrita Spa.

City Hall, Map p.290 C2 **6**

Scarlet Boutique Hotel

www.thescarlethotel.com

6511 3333

Daring, funky and individualistic, this small boutique hotel offers five-star quality and style. Facilities include an outdoor Jacuzzi and a gym, but mostly, the action is left for you to create in the indulgently sexy bedrooms.

Chinatown, Map p.295 C3 **7**

The Sentosa Resort & Spa

www.thesentosa.com

6275 0331

Surrounded by tropical woodlands and close to the beach, The Sentosa is a deluxe resort offering an award-winning spa, two of Asia's best golf courses at Sentosa Golf Club, tennis courts, a gym, volleyball and pétanque.

HarbourFront, Map p.298 C3 **8**

Shangri-La Hotel
www.shangri-la.com
6737 3644
This famed hotel lives up to the hype. The extensive gardens, complete with waterfalls and exotic pools, have won numerous awards and the service is high. Facilities include a fitness centre, pools, Jacuzzi, and a sauna.
🚇 Orchard, Map p.281 F1 **9**

Singapore Marriott Hotel
www.marriott.com
6735 5800
The Marriott commands a spectacular view of the city and being placed in the busiest part of Orchard makes it ideal for leisure and business travellers. Facilities include meeting rooms, an outdoor pool, and The Retreat spa.
🚇 Orchard, Map p.282 B3 **10**

Swissôtel The Stamford
www.swissotel.com
6338 8585
In the centre of the CBD, this hotel, (previously the world's tallest), is located in Raffles City Shopping Complex. There are 16 restaurants and lounges, business facilities, two pools, six tennis courts and a spa.
🚇 City Hall, Map p.290 C3 **11**

Other Hotels

Five Star

Grand Hyatt Singapore	6738 1234	www.hyatt.com
Hilton Singapore	6737 2233	www.hilton.com
Meritus Mandarin	6737 4411	www.mandarin-singapore.com
Pan Pacific Hotel	6336 8111	www.panpacific.com
Royal Plaza on Scotts	6737 7966	www.royalplaza.com.sg
Shangri-La's Rasa Sentosa	6275 0100	www.shangri-la.com
Sheraton Towers	6737 6888	www.sheratonsingapore.com
The Oriental Mandarin	6338 0066	www.mandarinoriental.com

Four Star

Amara Hotel	6879 2555	http://singapore.amarahotels.com
Copthorne Orchid Hotel	6415 6000	www.millenniumhotels.com
Furama RiverFront Hotel	6739 6405	www.riverfront.furama.com
Meritus Negara	6737 0811	www.meritus-negara.com.sg
Novotel Clarke Quay	6338 3333	www.accorhotels.com
Orchard Parade Hotel	6737 1133	www.orchardparade.com.sg
The Elizabeth Singapore	6738 1188	www.theelizabeth.com.sg

Three Star

Albert Court Hotel	6339 3939	www.albertcourt.com.sg
River View Hotel	6732 9922	www.riverview.com.sg
Robertson Quay Hotel	6735 3333	www.robertsonquayhotel.com.sg
Summer View Hotel	6338 1122	www.summerviewhotel.com.sg
Treasure Resort	6271 2002	www.treasure-resort.com

Two Star

Dickson Court Hotel	6297 7811	www.dicksoncourthotel.com.sg
Fragrance Hotel	6844 7888	www.fragrancehotel.com
Hotel Bencoolen	6336 0822	www.hotelbencoolen.com

Hostels

In the last few years the increase in budget travel, along with the realisation of the economic potential afforded by backpackers, has created a niche of hostels and guesthouses catering for this market. They provide just the essentials: clean accommodation, decent service, security and internet access with prices starting from around $20 per person per night. Most are independently-run single establishments, though a few chains are beginning to emerge, most notably Fern Loft Backpacker Hostel (6449 9066, www.fernloft.com) and the Hotel 81 chain (6476 8181, www.hotel81.com.sg) that even offers two or four-hour rentals. Independents worth checking out include the New 7th Storey Hotel in the Colonial District (6337 0251, www.nsshotel.com) and Sleepy Sam's Bed & Breakfast (9277 4988, www.sleepysams.com) on Arab Street, which even has an inexpensive spa on site.

Campsites

Camping isn't encouraged as a form of accommodation in Singapore, but there's a choice of five parks on the mainland where overnight stays are allowed. On weekends, no permit is necessary, but weekday camping is allowed only in designated areas and a permit is required, issued daily and on the spot by park rangers patrolling (for a maximum of three consecutive nights).

For more details on these parks you can either call the National Parks Board (1800 471 7300), or check out their site; www.nparks.gov.sg. For further information on camping, see page 148.

Singapore **mini** Explorer

Bussorah Street, Kampong Glam

Exploring

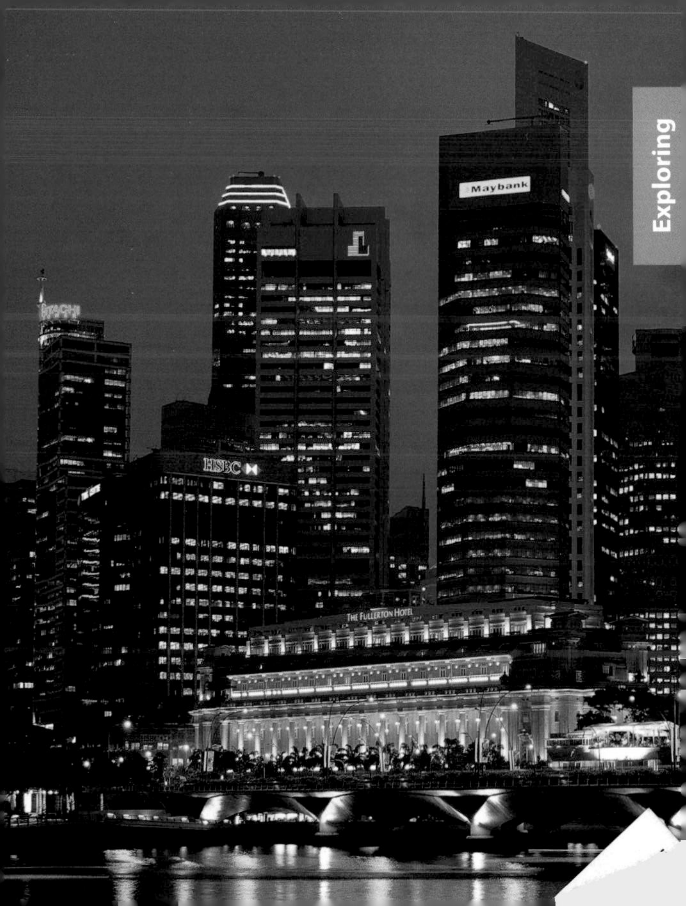
Maybank
HSBC
THE FULLERTON HOTEL

Explore Singapore

From the vibrant city centre to the peace of the outer islands, Singapore has something to offer every visitor to its unique shores.

For a nation of just 682 square kilometres, Singapore has had to take a tactical approach to gain its considerable prosperity. For visitors this means a compelling mixture of attractions, in a city that has been carefully planned to allow easy movement.

Singapore is famed for its diversity: leafy tracts of rainforest and manicured tropical gardens; gleaming malls and tall towers; shady riverside restaurant shophouses and bars; and all the rich colours and aromas of the ethnic quarters.

The city's best images begin with its most visible attractions. Start with the ethnic quarters of Chinatown, Little India and Arab Street, and enjoy the bustle of tradition and daily commerce. A detour down the back streets will present you with a number of hidden worlds away from the traffic and dust. Here the traditional multi-coloured shophouses provide a more human scale to the scenery and the mixture of businesses, from spice merchants, fabric sellers and herbalists to sidewalk cafes, provides a lot to see and take in. Unique to Singapore, shophouses are two or three storey-high buildings that originally had a shop on the ground floor, with living quarters above.

Many have now been converted and they've become sought-after spaces for living, playing and exhibiting art or

Asian Civilisation Museum

fashion in. There are Indian and Chinese temples and Muslim mosques here, often side by side, and they're open for respectful visitors to explore.

The centre of the city is defined by a zone known for its heritage, and dotted with early 20th century schools and convents now used as museums and leisure areas. One version of the city's heritage walk stretches roughly from the leafy escapes of Fort Canning, down past the Singapore Art Museum, Raffles Hotel and the grass-lined Padang to the riverfront. Thanks to a project to light up the city's trees and building, this makes particularly good exploring in the cool of the evening.

At a Glance

Heritage Sites

Temples & Mosques

Museums & Art Galleries

Main Attractions & Sights

Exploring

At a Glance

CBD, Marina Bay & Suntec

Amazing views, world-class malls and waterside entertainment are all on offer when you go downtown.

Depending on where you see them from, Singapore's two imposing high-rise clusters of the Financial District and Suntec City appear to rise dramatically out of the Singapore River, the shophouse bars of Boat Quay or the attractive shop frontages of North Bridge Road in Chinatown. The financial and corporate pulse of the city beats here, yet the centre of each cluster is relatively small – one encompassing Raffles Place and Shenton Way, the other at the north-eastern edge of the CBD on three blocks of reclaimed land around Suntec.

It used to be that the high-rise clusters hugging either side of the harbour mouth had little to offer for leisure, save a little fishing. But this has changed in the last decade, thanks to major urban redevelopment that has made the harbour and river mouth an entertainment focal point. This has included the construction of the Esplanade and One Fullerton developments – and has continued inland past Empress Place and along the Singapore River with the continuing upgrade of the city's riverside areas. In local marketing speak, the river is rapidly becoming a place to 'live, work and play' once again. Shopping is a big draw too with Suntec City (p.178) still popular. Further attractions are being built across the water in Marina South. These include a revolving wheel called The Singapore Flyer, landscaped waterfront gardens and tourist development that will house one of the nation's first two casinos. A project that's due to be completed in 2007 is a dam across the Marina Channel that will turn the bay into a fresh water reservoir and a year-round arena for events and sports like powerboat racing.

*For **restaurants and bars** in the area, see p.199.*

Esplanade – Theatres on the Bay

6828 8377

1 Esplanade Drive, Marina Bay   www.esplanade.com

Nicknamed 'the durians' by Singaporeans for the way its roof structure resembles two durian halves laid flat, the $600 million Esplanade waterfront complex is Singapore's unofficial headquarters for performing arts and the place to watch broadway musicals, concerts, plays and dance performances. There are 45 minute tours of the venue on week days at 11:00 and 14:00 and 11:00 on weekends. Tickets cost $8 for adults and $5 for children under 12. 🚇 City Hall, Map p.291 D4 **1**

Fountain of Wealth

6295 2888

5 Temasek Blvd, Suntec   www.suntec.com.sg

The world's largest fountain, it occupies the centrepiece of the traffic island in Suntec City, although most of it is underground. Made of bronze, it has a ring of 66 metres and a base area of 1,683 square metres. Suntec City's design, like much of Singapore, is built in accordance with feng shui and the buildings represent the fingers and thumb of a left hand poking out of the ground, with the fountain forming the hand's palm. While the water is low, visitors walk around the fountain for luck and at night there is a laser show. 🚇 City Hall, Map p.291 E2 **2**

The Fullerton Singapore

6733 8388

1 Fullerton Square, CBD www.fullertonhotel.com

Named after Robert Fullerton, the first governor of the Straits Settlements, this hotel used to be the General Post Office and cost over $4 million when it was built in 1928. The revolving beacon was added to the roof in 1958 and is now an Italian restaurant, San Marco (p.209). The Post Office moved in 1996, and after a $340 million restoration the Fullerton opened in 2000 as a landmark hotel. 🚇 Raffles Place, Map p.296 C1 **3**

Lau Pa Sat

Boon Tat St, CBD

Best known as Lau Pa Sat ('old market' or, in Malay, 'iron market'), Telok Ayer Market is a must-visit for its atmosphere, aromas and range of hawker food. The attractive octagonal cast iron building was made in Glasgow, and reassembled here in 1894 to become the city's second market. Originally extending over the sea, as land reclamation took place it became a general market until the 1970s. In 1986, it became a hawker centre (see page 201). 🚇 Raffles Place, Map p.296 B3 **4**

Marina City Park

1800 471 7300

Off East Coast Parkway, Marina Bay www.nparks.gov.sg

Marina City Park is a 26.2 hectare park right at the bottom of the city, which means it's well-located for good views of the skyline. Set on reclaimed land, it has a two-tiered pond with a fountain that spouts water to a height of 18m. There are three large open spaces where major events can be held, and you can wander among sculptures. 🚇 Marina Bay, Map p.297 F3 **5**

If you only do one thing in...

CBD, Marina Bay & Suntec

A sunset meal at Hai Tien Lo (p.200) means you can soak up the finest sky-high views.

Best for...

Eating: Fatman Satay's hawker food at the Lau Pa Sat market (p.201).

Drinking: The outdoor seating at hip bar Balaclava (p.205) is a prime people-watching spot.

Sightseeing: Walk around the Fountain of Wealth (p.57), you never know your luck.

Shopping: Mall heaven with Suntec City (p.178) linked to Raffles City Shopping Centre (p.177), together offering literally hundred of outlets.

Outdoor: See public art and stunning views at Marina City Park (p.58).

Clockwise from top left: CBD, People of the River sculptures, Parliament House & CBD

Chinatown

A mixture of temples, markets, specialist shops and tourist traps, Chinatown is a vibrant commercial and cultural area.

With bustling shops and great hawker food, Chinatown lies within walking distance of the Financial District. Centred around South Bridge Road and spanning several blocks either side, Chinatown is in fact a series of less distinct areas, each with its own appeal. Offering noisy open air markets and festive decorations here in the weeks leading up to Chinese New Year, foot reflexology and a variety of massages at other times, Chinatown's many faces reflect traditional and modern Singapore life at the same time – which is very much a reflection of how the country's people embrace these different facets of their environment in their everyday lives.

Enter Chinatown by train and you'll rise up from the underground onto Pagoda Street to see shophouses looming above you on either side. Search among the hawker stalls at Maxwell Food Centre (p. 208) and you'll find gems, but you may still have to wade through a good deal of tat first. The success of the area is that the authorities have been able to limit the amount of traffic flowing through it. Someone may have to look at the quality of offerings and the touts next.

Socially and architecturally speaking, there are many Chinatowns – the design houses, cosy cafes and bars of Club Street and Duxton Hill; North Bridge Road's expanses of 1970s malls and retail oddities; colourful Tanjong Pagar with its eclectic range of bridal salons by day, gay bars by night. Beyond this are the fancy residences and hushed elegance of the Tanjong Pagar conservation area, and then, if you double back toward the Outram Park MRT station, you'll stumble into streets that sport a combination of brothels, boutique hotels and bars. Whichever part of Chinatown you're in though, you'll find wonderful local food – oily, cheap, strange and delicious.

Spend a good half day here getting purposefully lost. The magic here often starts where you hadn't been planning on looking.

*For **restaurants and bars** in the area, see p.207. For **shopping**,* *see p.168.*

Chinatown Heritage Centre

6325 2878

Pagoda St, Chinatown   www.chinatownheritage.com.sg

An air-conditioned escape from the heat, this is a three-story museum within three restored shophouses, just a short walk from the Chinatown MRT station. Get up close with recreated scenes from early Chinatown including a teahouse, a prostitute's boudoir and a Chinese funeral. Entry costs $8.80 for adults, $5.30 for children. ☐ Chinatown, Map p.295 F2 **6**

Jamae Chulia Mosque

218 South Bridge Rd, Chinatown

Jamae Chulia is a national monuments, and one of three Islamic heritage buildings in Chinatown that were erected by early immigrants. The other two are Al-Abrar Mosque and Nagore Durgha on Telok Ayer Street. The entrance gate is distinctively South Indian, while the two prayer halls and the shrine are built in neo-classical style. During Hari Raya Haji, the Festival of Sacrifice, the mosque sacrifices goats and sheep in remembrance of Prophet Abraham and distributes the meat to the poor.

☐ Chinatown, Map p295-F2 **7**

The Caged Birds

Most days, and especially on Sundays, if you're in Tiong Bahru you'll witness shrilly tweeting birds in ornamental cages, singing while their owners gather to chat. Nearby coffee shops keep everyone plied with refreshments. This scene used to be a common sight in Singapore so catch it while you can.

The Singapore City Gallery

6221 6666

45 Maxwell Rd, Chinatown   www.ura.gov.sg/gallery

Run by the Urban Redevelopment Authority, the City Gallery boasts a 100 square metre architectural model of the city, as well as two floors of exhibits detailing the country's transformation to the bustling and economic powerhouse it is today. Well worth an orientation visit when you first arrive in Singapore. Admission is free. ▣ Tanjong Pagar, Map p294 A4 **8**

Sri Mariamman Temple

6223 4064

244 South Bridge Rd, Chinatown

The island's oldest Hindu place of worship stands in the heart of Chinatown, and is still very much in use today. Do remove your shoes before entering and hand over your 'tourist tax' to the caretaker at the door. Your entry will cost $3 for the use of a camera or $6 for a video camera. Tourist are asked not to enter the main worship area. Open daily from 07:00 to 12:30 and 18:00 to 20:30. ▣ Chinatown, Map p.295 F2 **9**

Thian Hock Keng Temple

6423 4616

158 Telok Ayer St, Chinatown

Thian Hock Keng, the oldest Chinese temple in Singapore was initially built in 1819 and rebuilt in 1839, the temple was built in southern Chinese style, with a grand entrance featuring a high step in front. Guarding the doors are tigers, lions and door gods. The temple underwent a major renovation in 2000. Its most attractive feature, a calligraphic panel from the Emperor of China, Guang Xu of the Qing Dynasty, dates to 1907. ▣ Tanjong Pagar, Map p.296 A3 **10**

If you only do one thing in...
Chinatown

Enjoy a relaxing reflexology session followed by a curbside meal (p.208).

Best for...

Eating: Maxwell Food Centre (p.208) is open 24 hours and is ideal for a tasty, exotic meal any time of the day.

Drinking: A chaotic drink in the noisy Crazy Elephant (p.210) is the perfect end to a hectic day.

Sightseeing: Go back in time at the Chinese Heritage Centre (p.64).

Shopping: Search through the generic tat to find some real bargains – stock up on silk and Chinese trinkets. See page 168.

Outdoor: Simply wandering around the buzzing streets is a feast for all the senses.

Top: Covered markte in Chinatown, Bottom: Chinese lanterns

Colonial District

The historical heart of Singapore has some superb spaces, famed heritage sites and is home to the Raffles Hotel, so what are you waiting for?

At the base of Orchard Road leading to the harbour and river's edge is the colonial or civic district. Singapore's most noted historic buildings are found in a five-block square. From cathedrals to forts, hotels to convents, the buildings here reflect Singapore's new concern for conserving its heritage, and provide a soulful link with the past. Home to colonial buildings, museums and parks, the area has witnessed many of the country's landmark moments in history. While necessity dictates that the historical buildings often sit alongside new office blocks and shopping centres, the government has still managed to protect a good number of its most attractive structures.

In some cases inspired urban redevelopment has seen buildings being given a new life – the Singapore Art Museum (p.75) being a notable example. In other cases, such as the Raffles Hotel (p.74), historic buildings were rebuilt and expanded in award-winning style.

Development wins occasionally too, as was the unfortunate case with the tree-lined park on Bras Basah Road that is now the site of the new and rather ugly Singapore Management University. Put this aside though when you explore the city's heritage buildings – your presence and

Left: The Art House, Right: St Andrew's Cathedral

feedback will help to preserve them further, as will the district's dual purpose as a training and tourism centre. *For **restaurants and bars** in the area, see p.213.*

Armenian Church of St Gregory the Illuminator

6334 0141

60 Hill St, Colonial District

Singapore's first permanent place of worship was built in 1835 in neo-classical style by George Coleman. The grounds include graves of several Sarkies (although not the two Sarkies brothers who opened Raffles Hotel), and Agnes Joaquim, the Armenian who discovered Singapore's national flower, the Vanda Miss Joaquim. The church is open on Mondays to Fridays, 09:00 to 17:00, and 09:00 to 12:00 on Saturdays. 🚇 City Hall, Map p.290 B3 **11**

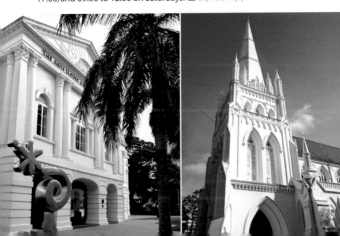

The Arts House

6332 6900

1 Old Parliament Lane

www.theartshouse.com.sg

Singapore's oldest government building was reopened in 2004 as a superb riverside venue for art exhibits, plays, movie screenings and corporate events. Opening hours are from 10:00 to 20:00 Mondays to Fridays, 11:00 to 20:00 on Saturdays. The current Parliament House is just next door, and sessions are open to the public (just take your passport or other identification along). ⬛ Raffles Place, Map p.290 C3 **12**

The Battle Box

6333 0510

Fort Canning Park, Colonial District

An interesting stop for history buffs and World War II veterans, the Battle Box was the British Malaya Command's underground operations centre during the war. You can only enter on a guided tour but these are conducted every half hour. For 30-40 minutes you'll be taken nine metres underground to what was the Allied Forces' largest military operations complex in Singapore. Tours cost $8 for adults, $5 for children, and are available Tuesdays to Sundays from 10:00 to 18:00 (the last tour is at 17:00). ⬛ Dhoby Ghaut, Map p290 A2 **13**

Bugis Street

Colonial District

Bugis Street is of more interest for its colourful past than its present day shopping and food outlets. In the mid 1960s this was the centre of much of the 'action' for western tourists. The area, with its transsexuals and transvestites, outdoor bars and food centres, was nicknamed 'Boogie Street' – and was once the subject of a Hong Kong movie. Little of this remains though, and apart from a night market and the large Bugis Junction mall it's now a fairly soulless spot.

Highlights nearby include the fabulously gothic-looking Park View building, whose imposing exterior and lavish lobby wouldn't look out of place in Gotham City, or 1930s Manhattan. 🚇 Bugis, Map p.285-D4 **14**

Cathedral of the Good Shepherd
4 Queen St, Colonial District

6337 9879
www.veritas.org.sg

Singapore's oldest Catholic building, built between 1843 and 1847, was administered by French missionary Jean-Marie Beurel. Father Beurel also established St Joseph's Institution, now the Singapore Art Museum. A quick visit is interesting, because while the condition of the building is fading, it retains a more original feel than many of Singapore's restored buildings. 🚇 City Hall, Map p.290 B2 **15**

Chijmes
30 Victoria Street, Colonial District

6332 6273
www.chijmes.com.sg

Having spent 131 years as the Convent of the Holy Infant Jesus, Chijmes on Victoria Street is now an atmospheric complex of restaurants, bars and venues (including Pizzeria Giardino, p.215 and Table 108, p. 216). The walled compound and grass lawns make it ideal for jazz events and recitals. The attractive chapel and Caldwell House are are both national monuments, and 40 minute tours run on weekdays from 11:00 to 15:00, costing $6 per person, including afternoon tea. 🚇 Lavender, Map p290 C2 **16**

Fort Canning Park

6332 1200

Bottom of Orchard Rd, Colonial District   www.nparks.gov.sg

The only elevated park in the area, Fort Canning was once known as Bukit Larangan – the Forbidden Hill. For families and history and nature lovers, Fort Canning is an easy place to spend a pleasant afternoon. It features the Battle Box (p.70), the shrine to Sultan Iskandar Shah, the last ruler of the ancient kingdom of Singapura and a fragrant Spice Garden built on the site of Raffles' former botanical garden.

🚇 Clarke Quay, Map p.290 A2 **17**

National Museum of Singapore

6332 3659

93 Stamford Rd, Colonial District   www.nationalmuseum.sg

Previously the Singapore History Museum, this cultural attraction reopened in December 2006. The new museum offers a more interactive look at Singapore's history, with light and sounds displays, perfect for hands-on kids and information-hungry adults alike. Alongside its exhibition programme, the museum also offers year-round activities and festivals. 🚇 Dhoby Ghaut, Map p.290 B2 **18**

The Padang

6736 6622

St Andrew's Rd & Connaught Drive, Colonial District

This patch of grass now plays host to everything from the annual festive Chinggay Parade to Linkin Park concerts, but during World War II, Japanese occupying soldiers herded the island's Europeans to the Padang, before marching them on foot to Changi Prison. Its use for more frivolous activities is still an important part of Singapore life: in the colonial days people would gather at a corner named Scandal Point to swap gossip, and today it's still the place to watch football and rugby. 🚇 City Hall, Map p.290 C4 **19**

Raffles Hotel
6337 1886
Beach Rd, Colonial District
www.raffleshotel.com

Opened originally as a 10 room colonial bungalow in 1887, Raffles soon became a home away from home for travellers, documented in the works of writers like Joseph Conrad and Somerset Maugham. Following an extensive $160 million restoration project, Raffles is once again a must do for travellers, even if all you do is have a Singapore Sling in the Long Bar (p.215) or high tea in the Tiffin Room (p.216).

Its small but fascinating Hotel Museum (free of charge, open daily from 10:00 to 19:00), Bar and Billiard Room, and Jubilee Hall are all open to the public, as are 70 shops and restaurants within the complex (a dress code does apply – so no shorts and sandals). 🚇 City Hall, Map p.291 D2 **20**

The Merlion

Designed by Fraser Brunner in 1964, The Merlion has become a trademark symbol for the city. It's a statue with a head of a lion and the body of a fish, inspired by the story of the discovery of Singapore by the legendary Sang Nila Utama who saw a lion while hunting on the island. There are five official Merlions, with the original at the mouth of the Singapore River. China also has many imitation Merlions dotted about its housing estates and commercial areas.

Singapore Art Museum

6332 3222

71 Bras Basah Rd, Colonial District   www.nhb.gov.sg/SAM

A former Catholic boys' school, the SAM is a good place to spend a couple of hours. It has 13 galleries and resident works include those of Filipino artist Ramon Orlina and US artist Dale Chihuly. The museum also has a cafe and gelataria. Entrance fees are $3 per adult, $1.50 per child and SAM is open from 12:00 to 18:00 on Mondays, from 09:00 to 21:00 on Fridays and from 09:00 to 18:00 on other days. 🚇 Dhoby Ghaut, Map p.290 B1 **21**

Singapore Philatelic Museum

6337 3888

23B Coleman St, Colonial District   www.spm.org.sg

Housed in the former Methodist Book Room Building and dating from around 1895, this may not have broad appeal but it is an interesting stop for those keen on stamp collecting. The museum has rare stamps, interactive displays and stamp designing activities for kids. Entry is $2 for adults, $1 for kids. 🚇 Clarke Quay, Map p290 A3 **22**

St Andrew's Cathedral

6337 6104

Coleman St, Colonial District   www.livingstreams.org.sg/sac

The elegant St Andrew's is one of the most beautiful churches in Singapore. It is in fact the third church to have been built on this site. Work on the present neo-Gothic cathedral was begun by lieutenant colonel Ronald MacPherson in 1856 using convict labour from India, and completed in 1861. The Visitor Centre has artefacts, memorials to soldiers, pictures and a video of its history. It is open daily and guided tours available on request. 🚇 Clarke Quay, Map p.290 C3 **23**

If you only do one thing in...
Colonial District

Have a refined afternoon and take in an exhibition at Singapore Art Museum (p.75) before high tea at Raffles Hotel (p.74).

Best for...

Eating: Chjimes (p.71) has some outstanding restaurants including Table 108 (p.216), all set in magical surroundings.

Drinking: The heady heights and slanting floor at the New Asia Bar & Grill (p.218) will make it a night to remember.

Sightseeing: The National Museum of Singapore (p.73) is a fun learning experience for everyone.

Shopping: The wide variety of shops and boutiques at Raffles City Shopping Centre (p.177) provide upmarket respite from the heat.

Outdoor: Find your own patch of green in Fort Canning Park (p.73).

Top: Cathedral of the Good Shepherd, Bottom: Singapore Philatelic Museum

East Coast

Breezy beach parks and fresh seafood provide the perfect antidote to the frantic city pace, so soak up the sun and relax.

With a little more space and perhaps a more laidback attitude to life than the city centre, the East Coast has the added benefit of ready access to the beach. And such a small island, nothing is really that far away – despite what some may say.

While the West Coast is more industrial and shipping-orientated, the East Coast is very much the leisure coast of Singapore, and the East Coast Park (right) in particular offers a long stretch of perfect coastline for running, cycling or just enjoying the sea breeze.

There are also some excellent places for food; whether it's chilli crab near the beach or local food in some of the city's oldest neighbourhoods, like historic Geylang and Katong. These are traditional Malay and Peranakan neighbourhoods, and outside of festive seasons like Hari Raya, they are also refreshingly quiet. *For **restaurants and bars** in the area, see p.221.*

Changi Chapel & Museum   6214 2451
1000 Upper Changi Rd North, Changi www.changimuseum.com
This evocative museum commemorates the Allied prisoners of war, and Singapore's experience of World War II through the eyes of different groups and races. The small but well-stocked museum features the remarkable Changi Murals,

made by imprisoned women to secretively let the men know they were alive. There is also a replica of the original Changi Prison chapel here, as the original site is still used for mainstream prison activities. ◼ Pasir Ris, Map p.277 E2

East Coast Park
All along the East Coast

1800 471 7300
www.nparks.gov.sg

Built on reclaimed land, the East Coast Park is one of Singapore's best and most enjoyed parks, with an 11 kilometre stretch of seafront. Popular at weekends, there are several bird sanctuaries, a popular sea sports club where you can hire windsurfers, nice breezy bars, hawker centres and restaurants. You can rent bikes and rollerblades for the car-free asphalt track. Along the way you'll find a waterpark; the Big Splash complex, and The Marine Cove Recreation Centre; an outdoor leisure complex offering bowling, squash and mini golf. In the evenings the East Coast Seafood Centre is a great place to enjoy fresh pepper crab alfresco. ◼ Tanah Merah, Map p.277 E3

Escape Theme Park
1 Pasir Ris Close, Pasir Ris

6581 9112
www.escapethemepark.com

If it's a traditional family theme park you're after, then Escape Theme Park delivers a good few hours of family noise, fun and splashes. It's an old school attraction with reliable favourites like a haunted ride, rollercoasters, a waterpark, ferris wheel, plane ride and bumper boats. Open on weekends and over school and public holidays from 10:00 to 20:00. Tickets cost $16.50 for adults, $8.30 for children or $40 for a family pass. ◼ Pasir Ris, Map p.277 E2

Johore Battery

6546 9897

Cosford Rd, Changi · www.visitsingapore.com

During WWII the British believed, given the strength of the
Japanese navy, that any attack on Singapore would come
from the sea. They built fortifications all around the south,
west and east coasts of the island, the pride of which was the
Johore Battery. Built in 1939, the site consists of a labyrinth
of tunnels used to store ammunition. Johore Battery was the
largest outside of Britain during WWII, and was kept a secret
until it was rediscovered in 1991. 🚇 Pasir Ris, Map p.277 F2

Katong Antique House

6345 1220

208 East Coast Rd, East Coast

Katong Antique House, which is linked to the local Peranakan
heritage association, has a fascinating collection of goodies
ranging from antiques and traditional ceramics, to beaded
slippers and wedding costumes. And if you call in advance
you can arrange for a Peranakan tea or a meal to be served to
you. Open from 11:00 to 18:00. Map p.277 E3

Pasir Ris Park

1800 471 7300

Pasir Ris Rd, Pasir Ris · www.nparks.gov.sg

Pasir Ris Park spans 71 hectares, including six hectares of
preserved mangroves. Boardwalks lead into the mangrove
forests, where you can view mud crabs, mudskippers and, yes,
mangrove trees. A three-storey bird watching tower gives you
a great vantage point for spotting the many bird species. The
park has a number of facilities like playgrounds, a cycling track,
barbecue pits and seafood restaurants. 🚇 Pasir Ris, Map p.277 E2

Wild Wild Wet

1 Pasir Ris Close, Pasir Ris

6581 9112

www.wildwildwet.com

The king of water parks in Singapore is Wild Wild Wet, which is part of the Escape Theme Park (p.79). The highlight is Ulah-Lah, billed as the first raft slide in south-east Asia and the closest thing to white water rafting that Singapore can offer. Younger children can play in the Professor's Playground with its slides, ladders, water cannons and fountains. Tickets cost $12.90 for adults, $8.80 for children and the park is open from 13:00 to 19:00 on weekdays and 10:00 to 19:00 on weekends. 🚇 Pasir Ris, Map p.277 E2

Parks

The amount of greenery in Singapore surprises many visitors. As well as tracts of tropical virgin rainforest in the centre of the island, there are also numerous peaceful parks which provide a much-needed balance to the pace of the hectic city.

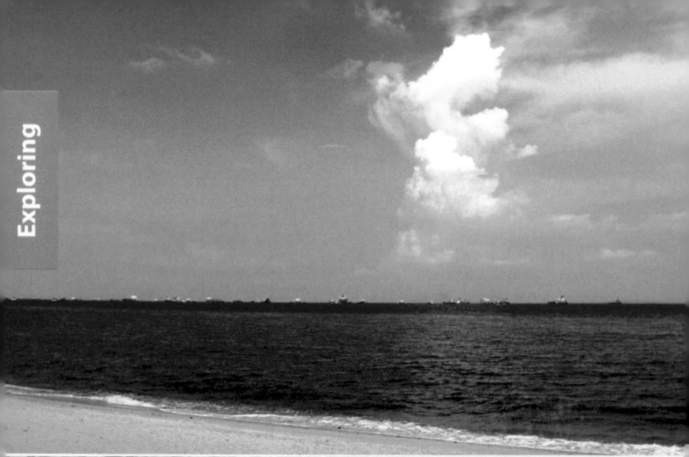

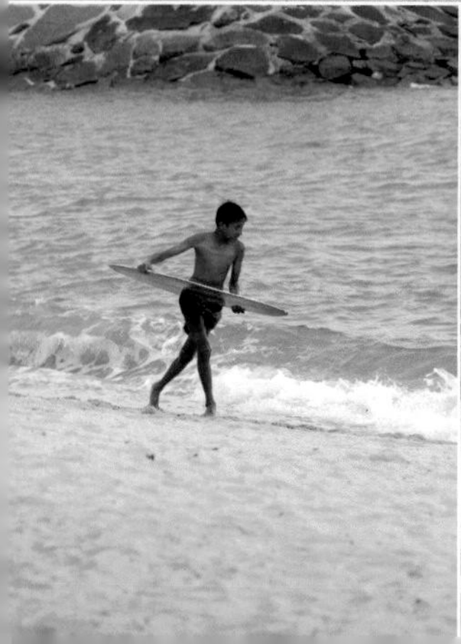

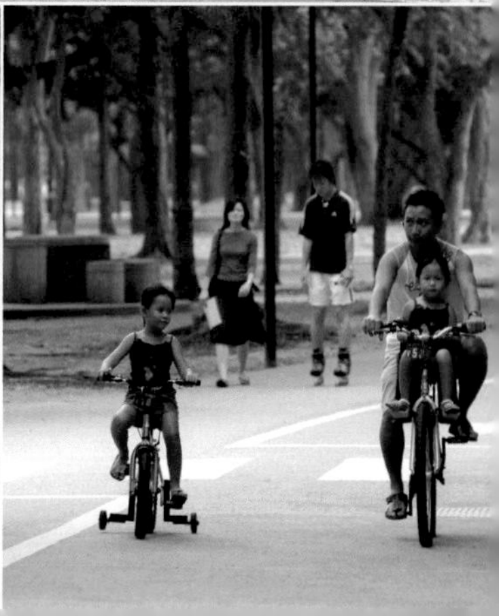

If you only do one thing in...
East Coast

Get your camera ready for the ornate Peranakan terrace houses on Koon Seng Road.

Best for...

Eating: Healthy, authentic Peranakan cuisine at Guan Hoe Soon Restaurant (see p.221) has been a favourite for generations.

Drinking: A cold beer with fresh seafood must be one of life's most simple pleasures. Try Jumbo Seafood (p.221) for white pepper crab.

Sightseeing: Even the most dedicated history fans will learn something new at Johore Battery (p.80).

Outdoor: The choice of activities at East Coast Park (p.79) will put some colour in your cheeks.

Top: Beach on East Coast, Bottom: East Coast Park

Little India & Arab Street

These ethnic districts have their own identity, not to mention some outstanding food and unusual views that add a new dimension to Singapore.

Culturally, Little India is one of the richest districts in Singapore, offering you experiences ranging from savouring fish-head curry and masala tea along Racecourse Road to getting a henna tattoo or visiting a parrot fortune teller. Whether it's due to fear, respect or a little of both, Little India has retained an identity all its own and a sense of independence that goes beyond simply being a cultural heart for South Asians. This is partly because the place hasn't yet been over-themed or dressed up.

Apparently Little India developed around a former settlement for Indian convicts. Its location on the Serangoon River made it attractive for raising cattle and it became known for its trade in livestock. As more immigrants moved in from Chulia Kampong – an area that had been put aside for Indian immigrants under the Raffles Plan of Singapore – and as other economic activity in Little India developed, it began to look like a real Indian town.

Such is the way in which a slice of urban Indian has been transplanted here that you could be wandering the streets of Madras or Hyderabad. Ironically, the district is vibrant in the same way as a 'Chinatown' is vibrant in the West; it's made all the more distinct by the stark differences all around it.

Arab Street and the Kampong Glam area remain relaxing and interesting areas to eat, explore and learn about the city's Malay roots. Under the Raffles Plan, Kampong Glam was set aside for the Sultan of Singapore and the Malay and Arab communities. This, and the number of important mosques in the district, means this area is also often referred to as the 'Muslim Quarter'. Two places particularly worth visiting are Sultan Mosque (p.89) and the Malay Heritage Centre (p.87).

While much of the Malay community later moved to Geylang and other suburbs, the area is still an important one for the community. It buzzes with activity during the fasting month of Ramadan, when many Muslims break their fast here, and buy food and traditional wares for the feast that follows, Hari Raya Puasa. The area is a great place to eat and explore, tucked nicely away from much of the bustle of the central city. Stroll around its famous textile shops, and check out the stores selling fishing tackle, jewellery and rattan furniture. Later, stop by one of the cafes for tea and to smoke a shisha pipe.

For restaurants and bars in the area, see p.225. For shopping, see p.168 and p.169.

DHL Balloon

6338 6877

Tan Quee Lan St, Bugis

For an aerial view of Singapore, try out the DHL Balloon. As the world's largest tethered balloon, it takes people 40 storeys up, where they can photograph or video the 360° view of the city below. The viewing platform is sturdy and you're able to walk around it easily. Tickets (with warnings that children and baggage are 'not allowed' to fall off the

balloon – which, rest assured, does have mesh safety barriers)
cost $23 for adults, $13 for children, and a ride lasts for 10
minutes. The balloon 'flies' every 30 minutes from 11:00 to
22:00 daily, weather permitting. ⬛ Bugis, Map p.291 D1 **24**

Leong San See Temple

6298 9371

371 Race Course Rd, Little India

A quiet and peaceful Taoist temple, its name translates
from Cantonese as Dragon Mountain Temple. Beautifully
decorated, it is dedicated to the Goddess of Mercy, Kuan Yin.
At the back of the temple there are hundreds of wooden
tablets bearing the names and photographs of the deceased,

and many parents bring their children here to pray for them before an image of Confucius. 🏠 Farrer Park, Map p.279 E1 **25**

Little India Arcade
Campbell Lane, Little India

The Little India Arcade is a narrow pathway through a cluster of restored shophouses, each of which is filled to the brim with Indian clothing, accessories and incense. There's also a rather good Indian sweet shop near the Serangoon Road entrance. The Indian Cultural Corner within the Arcade, which will give you a bit of an introduction to the area, is open from Mondays to Saturdays and admission is free. 🏠 Little India, Map p.284 C3 **26**

Malay Heritage Centre
85 Sultan Gate, Kampong Glam

6391 0450
www.malayheritage.org.sg

This former palace was built between 1836 and 1843 for Ali Iskander Shah, the last Sultan of Singapore. While there's little in the museum, you will find a replica kampong house upstairs, as well as daily performances of Malay dance and music. Open from Tuesdays to Sundays from 13:00 to 18:00 and from 10:00 to 18:00 on Mondays. Fees vary from free entry to the compound, to $8 for adults and $4 for children to attend a cultural show. 🏠 Bugis, Map p.285 F4 **27**

Sakaya Muni Buddha Gaya Temple
366 Race Course Rd, Little India

6294 0714

Popularly known as the Temple of 1,000 Lights, this Buddhist temple across the road from the Leong San See Temple, is dominated by a 15 metre-high Buddha. Inside the temple is a two-metre long footprint made of mother-of-pearl and said to be a replica of a huge footprint on Adam's Peak in Sri Lanka (which Muslims believe to be that of Adam, Hindus that of the god Siva and Christians that of St Thomas). And for 50 cents you can spin the wheel of fortune and have your fortune told. 🔲 Farrer Park, Map p.285 E1 **28**

Sri Srinivasa Perumal Temple

6298 5771

397 Serangoon Rd, Little India

One of the most important Indian temples in Singapore, Sri Srinivasa Perumal is the starting point for the annual walk to the Chettiar Hindu Temple during the Thaipusam Festival (see p.32). Built in 1855, it was originally a simple structure with a prayer hall and pond. Its impressive six-tier tower or gopuram was built in 1966. Major reconstruction of the temple took place in the 1990s. 🔲 Farrer Park, Map p.279 E1 **29**

Sri Veeramakaliamman Temple

6293 4634

141 Serangoon Rd, Little India

The goddess Kali, Lord Shiva's bloodthirsty consort who is portrayed as having many arms and hands, has always been popular in Bengal. This temple, built in 1855 by Bengali labourers, is dedicated to her. The doors are covered with little bells and devotees ask God to grant their requests by ringing the bells before entering. The temple's ceiling is rimmed with statues of Hindu gods, while the main shrine houses a black statue of Kali next to Ganesh and Murugan. 🔲 Little India, Map p.284 C2 **30**

Sultan Mosque

6293 4405

3 Muscat St, Kampong Glam

When Singapore was ceded to the British in 1819, part of the agreement was the use of Kampong Glam for their residences. With a grant from Raffles and the East India Company, Singapore's most important, and biggest, mosque was built in the area in 1825 then replaced a century later. The mosque has a large dome, prayer hall that accommodates 5,000 people, mosaic tiled walls with inscriptions from the Quran and a rug donated by a Saudi prince. While visitors may enter when a prayer session isn't taking place, they must be modestly dressed. Taking photographs of people in prayer is considered inappropriate. 🚇 Bugis, Map p.285 E4 **31**

Map p.285 E4

If you only do one thing in...

Little India & Arab Street

A trip to Sultan Mosque (p.89) will ensure your holiday snaps are something special.

Best for...

Eating: Take your pick from the streetside restaurants and enjoy the novelty of superb Indian food served on a banana leaf plate (p.225).

Drinking: This area isn't on the bar crawl route but you should still enjoy an evening with a mocktail or glass of lassi in hand at one of the many cafes.

Sightseeing: See Singapore from the air in the DHL balloon (p.85).

Shopping: Sim Lim Square is filled with competitively priced camera equipment (p.185).

Outdoor: Get happily lost in the backstreets before smoking some shisha at a sidewalk cafe.

Clockwise from top left: Textiles in Little India, DHL Balloon, Interior of Sultan Mosque

North & Central

Get active, get an education, get lucky at the races or just get a breath of fresh air in the island's green belt.

This area boasts numerous natural attractions worth visiting including Bukit Timah Nature Reserve (p.93) and MacRitchie Reservoir Park (p.94), not to mention the Sungei Buloh Wetland Reserve in the north-west which, in 2002, became the first wetlands reserve to have been gazetted in Singapore. A stopover point for migratory birds, it's 1.3 square kilometres of birding pleasure. Orchid enthusiasts will enjoy the Mandai Orchid Gardens, a short walk from the Singapore Zoo (p.97).

Kranji in the north makes a nice scenic drive (map p.276 C1). A military camp prior to the Japanese invasion, Kranji is now home to the Kranji War Cemetery and the memorial at 9 Woodlands Road. The Kranji War Memorial's walls are inscribed with the names of 24,346 British men and women from Singapore, Malaya, Java and Sumatra who died in the war.

Further along the winding road are a series of organic farms and lifestyle farms, perhaps the closest to 'alternative lifestylers' that Singapore has. Ivy Singh-Lim runs Bollywood Veggies, a lovely organic farm near Kranji that has short guided tours and a cafe that serves home-cooked Asian cuisine (made from organic ingredients, of course). Call them first before visiting (6898 5001) to let them know you're on the way.

For some outdoor amusement, dress up and head to the races at the Singapore Turf Club (see p.96). If it's more traditional culture you crave, Kong Meng San Phor Kark

See Temple (p.94), the largest Buddhist Temple in the country, is also in this area.

Bishan Park

1800 471 7300
Ang Mo Kio Ave 1, Central Singapore   www.nparks.gov.sg

Situated in the central area of the island, north of city, this is one of the country's biggest parks at 52 hectares. With its lakes and bridges, colourful shrubs and lush greenery it's also one of the most popular. It has a cycling track, children's playground, lake and shaded lawn and it's often the venue for live music events. People enjoy fishing, walking and picnicking in the grounds here. 🚇 Bishan, Map p.300 C3 **32**

Bukit Timah Nature Reserve

6468 5736
177 Hindhede Drive, Bukit Timah   www.nparks.gov.sg

Singapore and Rio de Janeiro are the only two cities in the world to include a significant area of primary rainforest within their boundaries. Just 12 kilometres from the city, the Bukit Timah and Central Catchment Nature Reserves are home to more than 840 flowering plants and over 500 species of animals, including butterflies. The 164 hectare reserve is said by world-renowned ecologist Dr David Bellamy to contain more plant species than the entire North American continentYou have the choice of taking the North View, South View or Fern Valley paths. Each is well-marked so you can wander on quietly, keeping a lookout for butterflies, monkeys and flying lemurs or the unique insect-eating pitcher plant. At the centre of the park is Bukit Timah Hill, Singapore's highest point at 164 metres above sea level. Map p.300 A3 **33**

Kong Meng San Phor Kark See Temple
88 Bright Hill Rd, Bishan

6453 4046
www.kmspks.org

Venerable Zhuan Dao began to build this monastery in 1921 for the many monks who arrived in Singapore and didn't have any lodging and it remains the largest Buddhist temple here. The monastery's main function is as a crematorium and you're likely to witness a funeral ceremony here any day of the week. There are also various halls to wander through in which you'll find Buddha in different guises. The Pagoda of 10,000 Buddhas has 9,999 images of Buddha lining the inside of its golden, cone-shaped stupa, with the final Buddha being the giant one inside the pagoda. Map p.279 D1 **34**

MacRitchie Reservoir Park
Central Catchment Nature Reserve

1800 471 7300
www.nparks.gov.sg

The Central Catchment Nature Reserve includes more than a square kilometre of primary rainforest. For a great nature walk in the reserve of between 3 and 11km, start at MacRitchie Reservoir Park, where boardwalks surround the scenic reservoir. Enjoy good views of the water and aquatic wildlife, and some unique flora including pitcher and ant plants. Used as arubber plantation in the 19th century, there still remain some rubber trees in the area.

Also worth trying out is the 250m aerial free standing suspension bridge that spans Bukit Piece and Bukit Kallang. Twenty-five metres above the ground at its highest point, it's a great place to watch the birds in the nearby canopy. Another way to enjoy the reservoir is to rent a kayak and go for a paddle. 🚇 Braddell, Map p.300 C4 **35**

Singapore Zoo

Singapore Night Safari

6269 3411
Singapore Zoo, Seletar   www.nightsafari.com.sg

Possibly the best attraction on offer, Night Safari at Singapore Zoo makes the zoo experience a serene and haunting one, taking advantage of the cooler night air and the fact that this is when many of the animals are awake and active. The 40 hectare forested park is only open at night and features 120 species. It's worth the extra price to pay for the tram that takes you along the eight geographical zones, and within inches of strolling antelopes and hyenas menacingly sniffing the air. Once the tram ride is done it's time to walk the trails, which allow you to stop and take your time at your favourite enclosures. These include the Mangrove Walk, where bats flap past frighteningly close to you. 🚇 Ang Mo Kio, Map p.300 A2 **36**

Singapore Turf Club

6879 1000
1 Turf Club Ave, Woodlands   www.turfclub.com.sg

Why not live it up with a day at the races? Racing is conducted on selected Fridays, Saturdays and Sundays every month and starts at 13:45. You can watch all the action on a large outdoor screen or take your pick from vantage points with or without air conditioning. Admission to the Lower Grandstand, the non air-conditioned public level, is $3, while the air-conditioned Upper Grandstand costs $7. You can gain admission to special areas like the @Hibiscus, which also allows access to the restaurant for $20 or the Gold Card Room for $15. Dress is smart casual and entry is restricted to those 18 or over. 🚇 Kranji, Map p.276 C1

Singapore Zoo

6269 3411
www.zoo.com.sg

80 Mandai Lake Rd, Seletar

Singapore Zoo has over 3,000 animals, representing 410 species housed on 28 hectares of greenery. Opened in 1973 beside the Upper Seletar Reservoir, the zoo's many programmes include the popular 'breakfast with the animals' where you can feed yourself and the animals at the same time. The zoo prides itself on its captive breeding projects, education programmes and open-style exhibits that use hidden barriers rather than the traditional cages. There are also some new interactive activities, including elephant rides. The zoo is a good two to three-hour meander – go in the early evening and take in Night Safari after dinner. 🚇 Ang Mo Kio, Map p.300 B1 37

Exploring

If you only do one thing in...
North & Central

Singapore Zoo (p.97), or the Night Safari (p.96), are some of Singapore's most popular attractions, and for very good reason.

Best for...

Eating: Make a reservation at Bollywood Veggies in Kranji (p.92) for some tempting organic fare.

Drinking: Splash out and get dressed up for an afternoon of sophistication at the races (p.96).

Sightseeing: See the tropical side to the city with the rainforest walks in Bukit Timah (p.93).

Outdoor: Pack a picnic and head to one of the tropical green spaces such as MacRitchie Reservoir Park (p.94) for some time out.

Orchard & Tanglin

With its restaurants, shopping and quick access to the MRT, this is the ideal place to find your bearings and to soak up the urban atmosphere.

When you arrive in Singapore, Orchard Road tends to be your first and most convenient stop. The Singapore Government estimates that Orchard Road is visited by three-quarters of the tourists who visit Singapore each year.

As the name suggests, the road was originally the site of nutmeg plantations, pepper farms and fruit orchards. Now this four-lane, each-way street is dominated by hotels and shopping malls. For more information on shopping in this area see page 170.

Emerald Hill (p.101) offers some of the only original shophouse architecture left. You'll see more colonial architecture at the Goodwood Park Hotel (p.101), the tower of which is a national monument and The Istana, the President's official residence (p.102).

Orchard Road connects with Tanglin at the top western end (for a step back in time of the outdoor variety, see the Singapore Botanic Gardens on page 102) and the Colonial or Civic District near the river at its far end. Scotts Road, which intersects Orchard, is the second main street in this district.

Orchard has a cluster of top-line hotels too, including Shangri-La, Marriott, Hilton, Grand Hyatt and Meritus Mandarin. As a result, there are also some big name restaurants, bars and night spots here that can offer a good night out.

*For **restaurants and bars** in the area, see p.229. For **shopping**, see p.170.*

Emerald Hill

Off Orchard Rd   www.landseer.com.sg/conservation

The only area of original shophouse architecture left in Orchard, the narrow streets around Emerald Hill and Peranakan Place offer a charming escape from the noise and traffic. Just off Orchard Road is a stretch of two-storey bars (p.240) with indoor and outdoor seating; stroll beyond these and you'll find an attractive terrace of Peranakan-style shophouses dating from the 1920s. The area includes Cuppage Road, named after William Cuppage who owned the nutmeg estate originally on the site. This small area of highly sought-after shophouse residences reflects a blend of Chinese-influenced architecture and art deco style. ⬛ Somerset, Map p.283 E4 **38**

Goodwood Park Hotel

6737 7411

22 Scotts Rd, Orchard   www.goodwoodparkhotel.com

Tucked into a hillside on Scotts Road, Goodwood Park was designed by J Bidwell, the architect most famously known for Raffles Hotel. Originally known as the Teutonia Club, a club for German expatriates, its construction and landscaping began in 1900. Its tower is now a national monument. Not nearly as grand as the restored Raffles complex, Goodwood nonetheless gives you a feel for the original colonial hotel. ⬛ Orchard, Map p.282 C1 **39**

The Istana

6737 5522
www.istana.gov.sg

Orchard Rd, Orchard

The President of Singapore's official residence, this national monument is open to the public on selected public holidays. The neoclassical building was completed in 1869 and, originally named Government House, was the official residence of Singapore's colonial rulers. The architecture's Victorian and Roman influences are complemented by Gothic, Malay and Chinese features. Lush grounds of over 100 acres are cared for by the Singapore Botanic Gardens and include several rare species of plants and an exclusive nine-hole golf course. A visit here is a chance to step briefly back in time to the colonial days. 🚇 Dhoby Ghaut, Map p.290 A1 **40**

Singapore Botanic Gardens

6471 7361
www.sbg.org.sg

1 Cluny Park Rd, Tanglin

Founded in 1859, the Botanic Gardens' grounds were originally used as a testing area for cash crops. A few blocks from the top or western end of Orchard, they now make up a fine 52 hectare expanse of landscaped tropical gardens and established trees. The gardens boast a collection of over 3,000 species of orchids, a mini rainforest trail and a spice garden, making them a superb place to walk, explore and picnic.

With several lakes and a hillside amphitheatre, the gardens are the venue for many concerts, including the free Singapore Symphony Orchestra events and there are a number of restaurants worth visiting within the grounds, including Halia (p.229). The gardens also house the National Parks Board's headquarters. Map p.280 A1 **41**

Orchard Road Skyline

If you only do one thing in...
Orchard & Tanglin

Take a stroll along the tree-lined boulevard window shopping (p.170), to work up an appetite for dinner.

Best for...

Eating: The Line (p.231) at the Shangri-La Hotel is the venue of choice for Singapore's chic food fans.

Drinking: The many upmarket hotels mean luxury bars are just a revolving door away.

Sightseeing: Bliss out on the traditional shophouse architecture on Emerald Hill (p.101).

Shopping: Retail heaven for window shoppers and serious spenders alike. It's time to dust off the credit card...

Outdoor: The Botanic Gardens (p.102) offer respite from this consumer's paradise and you might even catch a concert.

Clockwise from top left: Wisma Atria Shopping Centre, Orchard Road, Emerald Hill

Sentosa

From cable car rides to beach volleyball, underwater discoveries to laser shows, Sentosa is positioned as the city's leisure hotspot.

Ideal for a day of fun in the island's gardens and on the white, sandy beaches, the island is currently undergoing a transformation and 'grown-up' entertainment such as beach bars, new restaurants and destination spas have broadened the appeal. The good times here are easily accessible: simply drive over to the island, catch a taxi or hop on the cable car from HarbourFront or Mount Faber Park (p.120) .

Despite the ease of access, Singapore's 'leisure island' certainly feels different to Singapore proper, with its five-star hotels and fine dining restaurants. For information about any aspect of the island, visit www.sentosa.com.sg or call 1800 736 8672.

With a mixed offering of attractions – some hits, some misses – this resort and theme park island will keep you busy. There are a number of themed attractions that kids enjoy, including Underwater World (p.109), Dolphin Lagoon, the Sentosa Luge (p.108), the Magical Sentosa musical fountain laser show in the evening, and the Carslberg Sky Tower that gives you an aerial view of the island. There's also Fort Siloso (p.107), the free Nature Walk (livened up with plastic dragons), and Images of Singapore (p.107) which will transport you through the ages of Singapore's History.

Sentosa also boasts several resorts including Shangri-La's Rasa Sentosa Resort (p.108), the Treasure Resort (p.109) and The Sentosa Resort & Spa (p.108). Day guests are also welcome so you can truly get away from it all.

*For **restaurants and bars** in the area, see p.242.*

Fort Siloso

6275 0388
33 Allanbrooke Rd, Sentosa   www.fortsiloso.com

The British Government, well aware of Singapore's commercial and strategic value in its colonial empire, decided to build a number of coastal gun batteries in the 1880s, including Fort Siloso. Unfortunately, when it came to testing Singapore's defences against the Japanese in WWII, the gun emplacements meant the guns were all facing the wrong way.

Nevertheless, a tour of the fort today is worthwhile, providing you with quite an entertaining glimpse of the past. You can work your way through the tunnels and networks, look at interactive displays and even try out an obstacle course. The fort is open from 09:00 to 18:30 daily and entry costs $5 for adults, $3 for kids. 🚇 HarbourFront, Map p.298 A1 42

Images of Singapore

6275 0426
40 Cable Car Rd, Sentosa

An award-winning attraction, Images of Singapore begins with a short video of how the country's four main ethnic groups have contributed to one of the world's busiest trading ports. Then you walk through the exhibits filled with wax figures (some mechanised), documenting Singapore's history from its fishing village days, through WWII hardship to independence and on to the present. Visitors can learn about some of the festivals and customs of the Indians, Chinese, Eurasians and Peranakans. 🚇 HarbourFront, Map p.290 B2 **43**

Sentosa Luge & Skyride

1800 736 8672
Imbiah Lookout, Sentosa
www.sentosa.com.sg

Part go-cart, part toboggan, the luge is easy to manoeuvre and a quick ride down the 650m track. To get to the top, you take a trip on the Skyride, a chairlift which takes you over the treetops of Sentosa. Consider doing it in the morning or late afternoon unless you fancy catching some tropical sunshine on your way up. Children aged 3 to 6 can ride tandem with an adult. All rides include the Skyride and cost $8 for a single, $15 for two rides and $24 for a family pass of four rides. 🚇 HarbourFront, Map p.298-B2 **44**

The Sentosa Resort & Spa

6275 0331
2 Bukit Manis Rd, Sentosa
www.thesentosa.com

An elegant Beaufort Hotel on the cliffs in Sentosa Island, this property is the most recently renovated of the Sentosa resort hotels and boasts 214 suites, rooms and villas. It's also home to Spa Botanica (p.163), Singapore's first true destination spa where you can wander through a meditation labyrinth, have a steam or wallow in a mud pool! 🚇 HarbourFront, Map p.298 C3 **45**

Shangri-La's Rasa Sentosa Resort

6275 0100
101 Siloso Rd, Sentosa
www.shangri-la.com

Singapore's only beachfront resort, the Rasa Sentosa is perfect for a getaway with the kids and a number of quieter pursuits for parents; from a stroll through the extensive tropical gardens, to spoiling yourself at the Health Club & Spa. If you're feeling energetic there's also a climbing wall and beach volleyball on offer. There are 459 rooms, a swimming pool and two outdoor Jacuzzis. 🚇 HarbourFront, Map p.298 A1 **46**

Treasure Resort
23 Beach View, Sentosa

6271 2002
www.treasure-resort.com

An excellent example of colonial architecture, the Treasure Resort is strategically located beside the Merlion, close to Imbiah monorail station. It has 63 rooms with private balconies that overlook lush greenery, the sea or the Merlion itself. Try the Coffee House restaurant for a taste of the delicious local cuisine. After substantial renovation work in 2007 the resort will be rebranded in 2008 as the Mövenpick Treasure Resort Sentosa. 🚇 HarbourFront, Map p.298 B2 **47**

Underwater World
80 Siloso Rd, Sentosa

6275 0030
www.underwaterworld.com.sg

One of Sentosa's most popular sights, this attractive aquarium houses some 250 species of marine life from around the region. The highlight is the travelator – a 83 metre moving walkway that takes you through a tunnel filled with shoals of fish, rays, sharks and massive grouper that swim alongside and above you. The aquarium is particularly entrancing after 19:00, when they turn off the lights and equip visitors with torches to spot the critters with. Also worth a look is the Dolphin Lagoon with pink dolphins in regular shows throughout the day. 🚇 HarbourFront, Map p.298 B1 **48**

If you only do one thing in...
Sentosa

Take a scenic trip on the Skyride (p.108) and scream your way down again if you're brave enough.

Best for...

Eating: Il Lido (p.243) at Sentosa Golf Club offers an outdoor area and authentic Italian cuisine.

Drinking: See and be seen at KM8 (p.243), where the beautiful people drink, dance and laze the day away.

Sightseeing: Images of Singapore (p.107) will give you a unique insight into the ethnic mix in the city-state.

Outdoor: Choose from golf (p.156), the downhill luge (p.108), the beach or even the obstacle course at Fort Siloso (p.107) to get your fresh air fix.

Singapore River

Once crucial to Singapore's trading history, the river district now deals in good times, cultural enlightenment and an unexpected dash of G-force.

Arranged into Boat Quay, Clarke Quay and Robertson Quay, the river district was once the site of Singapore's earliest trading activities, and now hosts some of its finest dining activity. The best place to start and finish a walking and boat tour of the area is at the river mouth, at 1 Empress Place where the marble statue of Sir Stamford Raffles marks the spot where he first set foot in Singapore on 29 January 1819.

Visit the Asian Civilisations Museum (see p.114), the city's newest and most impressive museum, then stop for a drink at Empress Place to enjoy the view of Boat Quay and the high towers across the water, . Walk past the attractive Victoria Theatre & Concert Hall, built in 1862 – once a town hall, it's now a venue for shows from Rent to Buena Vista Social Club.

Carry on to the fabulous Fullerton Hotel (see p.58), once a post office and now a landmark hotel with some excellent drinking and dining options. At night, especially when a breeze is up, this is one of Singapore's most magical and evocative walks. Turn right, and walk towards Boat Quay, taking time to enjoy the brass People of the River sculptures that adorn both sides of the river. trader. Each gives a sense of the old life of the river. Stop for an ale at Harry's (p.251), once rogue trader Nick Leeson's favourite watering hole. Continue along Boat Quay past the two and three-storey shophouses

Anderson Bridge and The Fullerton

and cobbled paths. Now restaurant-central, these were once the homes and offices of the original Singapore traders.

Next, hop into a bumboat (so named as they would take goods from the aft of trading ships) for a tour of the remainder of the river. You'll pass under the Anderson, Elgin and Coleman bridges and follow the curve of the river around to Robertson and Clarke Quay. Clarke Quay (p.114) is now the new hotspot for nightlife and entertainment, while Robertson Quay was once used to store goods and now houses clubs, restaurants, hip hotels and outdoor bars. Also worth a look is the Singapore Tyler Print Institute (p.115). As the boat ride loops back, try and take it past The Fullerton (p.58) and out to sea – passing the mythical Merlion (p.74) spitting water at Esplanade Park.

*For **restaurants and bars** in the area, see p.245.*

Asian Civilisations Museum
6332 7798

1 Empress Place, Riverside   ww.nhb.gov.sg/ACM

The Asian Civilisations Museum is the pride of Singapore's museum scene. Located in the Empress Place Building, its three floors house 10 themed galleries that cover the history, religions, cultures and arts in Asia. Free tours are available in English, Japanese and Mandarin. Entry fees are $8 per adult, $4 per child and halfprice on Fridays. The Museum is open from 09:00 to 19:00 from Tuesday to Thursday, from 13:00 to 19:00 on Monday and from 09:00 to 21:00 from Friday to Sunday. 🚇 Raffles Place, Map p.296 C1 **49**

Chettiar Temple
6737 9393

15 Tank Rd, River Valley Rd

This Shaivite Hindu temple was built in 1984 to replace the one built by Indian chettiars, or money lenders. This temple is at its most colourful and exciting during the annual Thaipusam festival (around January and February), as the memorable procession ends up here. Open from 08:00 to 12:00 and from 17:30 to 20:30. 🚇 Dhoby Ghaut, Map p.289 F3 **50**

Clarke Quay

South of Singapore River   www.clarke quay.com.sg

Named after Sir Andrew Clarke, the second governor of Singapore, this used to be a strip of dilapidated 19th century warehouses run mostly by Chinese traders. Redeveloped into a less successful counterpart to Boat Quay in the early 1990s, its most recent makeover took two years to transform this waterfront strip into a popular night haunt, featuring eccentric (some say ugly) pods and lily pads. One place worth a visit is the Royal Selangor Pewter Museum (6268 9600) at 3A River Valley Road, which has a private collection of pewter items ranging from tobacco boxes to Chinese lanterns with lotus motifs. Map p.289 F3 **51**

G-Max Reverse Bungee
3E River Valley Rd, Riverside

6338 1146
www.gmax.com.sg

With a scarcity of suitable structures to bungee from in Singapore, the G-Max Reverse Bungee ride solves the problem. The capsule is anchored to the ground with bungee cords stretched to the top of two poles like a slingshot. The capsule is then released with you inside it – sending you hurtling into the sky at amazing speed, and some significant G-force. Try to catch the scenic view of the gaudy paintwork, lily pad umbrellas and gum drop railings of Clarke Quay below. Rides cost $35, $25 for students, and there is a height requirement of 1.2m. 🚇 Clarke Quay, Map p.290 F4 **52**

Singapore Tyler Print Institute
41 Robertson Quay, Riverside

6336 3663
www.stpi.com.sg

Established by American printmaker Kenneth E Tyler, the gallery holds printmaking exhibitions four times a year. Although Ken Tyler has returned to the States, his master printmakers remain and they collaborate with artists from around the world to make unique, limited edition prints, some of which are for sale here. The institute is open from 13:00 to 17:00 on Sunday and Monday and from 09:30 to 18:00 from Tuesday to Saturday. 🚇 Clarke Quay, Map p.289 D4 **53**

If you only do one thing in...
Singapore River

Put some comfortable shoes on and explore the area before discovering the thrilling nightlife (p.244).

Best for...

Eating: Saint Julien (p.249) was crowned Singapore Restaurant of the Year 2006 so sample its French cuisine and put it to the test.

Drinking: Harry's Bar (p.251) for the Crazy Hour and the longest happy hour in town.

Sightseeing: Boat Quay's shophouses are worth a look and a good photo opportunity.

Outdoor: All aboard a bumboat to see Singapore from the water. For tours see page 132.

Top: Clarke Quay, Bottom: Singapore River

West Coast

Cafe culture and green space abound in this bohemian hangout and you might find some snow too…

While Singapore's West Coast is dominated by its port activities, it has also a wide variety of interesting spots, from the expatriate enclaves and landed houses of Holland Village and Sixth Avenue, to the scenic stretch of Pasir Panjang and Jurong.

Reflections at Bukit Chandu in Pasir Panjang (6375 2519) is worth a visit if you're interested in military history. It is built in memory of the 1,400 soldiers of the Malay regiment who fought 13,000 Japanese soldiers in World War II.

Out in the Choa Chu Kang area are a number of farms where you can often spend a pleasant morning strolling around and maybe buy an ornamental fish, an exotic bird, hydroponic veggies, orchids or even a couple of frogs. Do make time to visit Jurong BirdPark (p.119), which is truly beautiful, and Mount Faber Park (p.120) will also give you great panoramic views of the island, as well as a great spot to dine and have a few drinks. For more on shopping in the arty and eclectic Holland Village, see page 169.

For something a little different, although not for the squeamish, take a visit to Haw Par Villa, an Asian mythology theme park (p.119). For some history and some cutting edge technology and fun, head to the Singapore Discovery Centre (p.120) or the Singapore Science Centre (p.120).

*For **restaurants and bars** in the area, see p.256.*

Haw Par Villa

6872 2780

262 Pasir Panjang Rd, Pasir Panjang

Built by the brothers behind the Tiger Balm company, Haw Par Villa is an Asian mythology theme park, which is currently pretty run down. For kitsch and novelty value though, it's probably worth a visit. The park includes nightmarish scenes of the 10 courts of hell within the stomach of a giant dragon. Not for the easily upset, the rides do depict very graphic torture scenes awaiting sinners in hell before reincarnation. Open daily from 09:00 to 19:00. Admission is free. Map p.278 B3 **54**

Jurong BirdPark

6265 0022

2 Jurong Hill, Jurong

www.birdpark.com.sg

A must-see, this park consists of 20 or so serene hectares on the western slope of Jurong Hill. With 8,000 birds from 600 species, it is among the largest bird parks in the world, and its presentation makes it a must-see, even if you're not a bird enthusiast. Built at a cost of $3.5 million in 1971, the park features The Waterfall Aviary, the world's largest walk-in aviary which is home to over 1,500 free-flying birds. The Jurong Falls within the aviary is said to be the tallest man-made waterfall in the world at 30 metres high. The World of Darkness is Asia's first nocturnal bird house, while Pelican Cove features seven species of these beautiful birds, including a unique underwater viewing gallery where birds scoop for fish at feeding time. There are also daily live performances including the All Star and Birds of Prey Shows. 🚇 Boon Lay, Map p.276 B3 **1**

Mount Faber Park

1800 471 7300
Opp Sentosa Island, Telok Blangah   www.nparks.gov.sg

Covered in secondary rainforest, Mount Faber is another of Singapore's fabulous green spaces. For 105 metre high panoramic views of the island – particularly good at night – you can visit the collection of restaurants and bars on Faber View, the hill opposite Sentosa Island. Recent redevelopments have seen a number of the bars become very stylish although the service is still rather lacking. Nevertheless, sitting on a breezy elevated hillside, overlooking 140 acres of forest, makes for a pleasant evening. 🚇 HarbourFront, Map p.278 C3 55

Singapore Discovery Centre

6792 6188
510 Upper Jurong Rd, Jurong   www.sdc.com.sg

There's some interesting cutting-edge fun and technology on display here, including interactive robots, a motion stimulator ride, a five-storey movie theatre that screens three-dimensional films and paintball using replica M4 Carbine guns. Tickets cost $9 for adults, $7 for children, and the centre is open from 09:00 to 19:00 from Tuesday to Sunday. 🚇 Boon Lay, Map p.276 B2

Singapore Science Centre

6425 2500
15 Science Centre Rd, Jurong East   www.science.edu.sg

Great for kids, the Singapore Science Centre offers special exhibits, such as the Lord of the Rings and Art of Star Wars, in addition to over 850 regular exhibits. It's easy to spend an entire day here, especially with things like The Millennium

Stimulator, which takes you through the heart of an active volcano. Visitors can also catch both Omnimax movies and Planetarium shows on a five-storey high screen that's set at 30° to the horizon. The centre is open from Tuesday to Sunday, from 09:00 to 19:00. 🏢 Jurong East, Map p.276 B2

Snow City

6560 1511

21 Jurong Town Hall Rd, Jurong   www.snowcity.com.sg

This hangar-sized fridge contains a three-storey high slope for those who would like to experience the cold (it's a chilly -5°C inside). You and the kids can spend half an hour at a time sliding down the slope on a tube. While the place is really quite gimmicky, it's fun when it's too hot outside or when the malls' appeal has worn thin. Ski and snowboarding lessons are also available. Opening hours are from 10:30 to 18:30 Tuesday to Sunday and from 09:00 to 20:00 on public and school holidays. Entry is $6 for adults, $3 for a child. 🏢 Jurong East, Map p.276 B2

West Coast Park

1800 471 7300

Pasir Panjang, West Coast   www.nparks.gov.sg

The 50 hectare West Coast Park was earlier a victim of land reclamation, but has subsequently been redeveloped. It has a number of features and facilities, including an adventure playground, bicycle obstacle course, fitness corner, a chess garden, a bird sanctuary and even foot reflexology facilities. Those seeking the beachfront within the park should enter via the West Coast Ferry Road or off the West Coast Highway and head to the north western corner of this long and narrow park. Map p.278 A2 56

If you only do one thing in...
West Coast

Burn some calories rollerblading in West Coast Park (p.121) then undo all your good work with some alfresco dining at Graze (p.258).

Best for...

Eating: Cafe culture abounds or check out Original Sin (p.258) for vegetarian Mediterranean cuisine and an impressive wine list.

Drinking: Local favourite Wala Wala Cafe Bar (p.259) is always packed, inside and out, guaranteeing a party atmosphere.

Sightseeing: Kids will love the Science Centre (p.120), especially the huge cinema screen.

Shopping: The bohemian vibe in Holland Village (p.169) makes it perfect for arts, crafts and clothing.

Outdoor: Jurong BirdPark (p.119) isn't just for ornithologists; it's a great day out for everyone.

Outer Islands

Escape to the outer islands, which are comparatively untouched by the modern lifestyles of mainland Singapore.

Kusu Island

The name in Malay (Pulau Tembakul) means Tortoise Island and legend has it that a giant turtle saved a Malay and Chinese sailor here by turning itself into a rock. The island is also a turtle sanctuary. From two tiny outcrops on a reef, the island has been enlarged and transformed into an island holiday resort of 85,000 square metres (but does not currently offer accommodation). The island has a popular Chinese temple, Da Bo Gong, and its hilltop hosts three Malay kramats, or shrines of saints dating from the 19th century.

Many devotees climb the 152 steps leading to the kramats to pray and Taoists make an annual pilgrimage to the Tua Pekong Temple here during the ninth lunar month. A daily ferry service leaves the Sentosa Ferry Terminal for Kusu Island and the trip takes about 30 minutes. See www.nparks.gov.sg for more details or call 1800 471 7300.

Pulau Ubin

Pulau Ubin, which can be reached by ferry from the Changi Village jetty, has a small community of villagers living in wooden houses but public pressure is keeping the island from being developed further. The only accommodation option for visitors is the upmarket Marina Country Club Ubin Resort.

You can still find a traditional village atmosphere here, along with granite quarries, coconut and rubber plantations, mangrove swamps, fish and prawn farms, and traditional fishing done with 'kelongs' or nets. Ubin is popular for walking, camping and cycling, with bikes available for hire at the village.

This virtually unspoilt reef around 5,000 years old, is a big attraction. A 10 minute bumboat ride takes visitors from Changi Village jetty to Pulau Ubin at an affordable cost. Marina Country Club Ubin Resort (p.126) is the main accommodation option for visitors and provides a variety of activities, whether you want to relax and unwind or be active and adventurous. See www.npark.gov.sg or call 1800 471 7300.

Marina Country Club Ubin Resort   6388 8388
Pulau Ubin   www.marinacountryclub.com.sg

Located on the edge of the Ketam Channel on Pulau Ubin, in a mangrove setting, the MCC Ubin Resort is just 15 minutes by boat from the Changi Village jetty on the mainland. The resort consists of one or two-roomed air-conditioned chalets with a colour TV, a fridge, a kettle and two skate scooters. There's also a recreation centre that offers abseiling, archery, rock climbing, kayaking, guided trekking and plenty of gear that you can hire if you fancy trying your hand at fishing, tossing a frisbee or an energetic game of volleyball. Map p.277 E2

St John's Island

Lying 6.5km to the south of the main island of Singapore, off the Straits of Singapore, this was the site of Raffles' anchorage before meeting the Malay chief of Singapore in 1819. Known locally as Pulau Sakuang Bendera, and reputedly haunted, it used to be a quarantine station for leprosy and cholera patients, political dissidents and heroin addicts. The remains of their housing litter the island and there's still a detention centre for illegal immigrants here, as well as the Marine Aquaculture Centre and Vipassana International (p.163), a meditation centre which offers courses for both stressed out residents and visitors to Singapore.

In 1975 though, the 39 hectare island was transformed into a tranquil getaway with lagoons, beaches, picnic grounds, trekking routes and soccer fields. With a host of flora and fauna, it's popular for weekend visits.

While the island houses the Tropical Marine Science Institute, the Agri-Food & Veterinary Authority of Singapore's Marine Aquaculture Centre, as well as a detention centre for illegal immigrants, visitors will probably prefer to stay in the Holiday Bungalow. This accommodates up to 10 people and has a kitchen, while the dormitories at the Holiday Camps take up to 60 people. You will need to arrange accommodation through the Sentosa Development Corporation (6275 0388, www.sentosa.com.sg). A daily ferry service leaves the Sentosa Ferry Terminal for the 45 minute trip to St John's Island.

The Sisters Islands

Lying to the south, off the Straits of Singapore, Big Sister's Island, also known as Pulau Subar Laut, is about 39,000 square metres in area, while Little Sister's Island, or Pulau Subar Darat, is roughly 17,000 square metres. The two are separated by a narrow channel that can be very dangerous to swimmers and divers.

The Sisters Islands' beaches and warm blue waters make snorkelling, picnicking and camping favourite activities here, and the islands have some of Singapore's richest reefs with sealife including giant clams, seahorses and octopus. The Southern Islands are soon to be developed and will ultimately feature high-end entertainment options, exclusive restaurants, resorts, spas and conference facilities.

Other islands around Singapore to look up and explore include Bukum, Hantu, Punggol Barat, Seletar, Semakau, Seringat and Tekong (all preceded by the word 'Pulau').

If you only do one thing in...
Outer Islands

Step back in time on Pulau Ubin (p.124) where you can experience a typical Singaporean village atmosphere from years gone by.

Best for...

Eating: Take a picnic to enjoy once you've found your land legs again.

Nature: Snorkel among the reefs around Sisters Islands (p.126), visit the turtle sanctuary on Kusu Island (p.124), or walk or cycle through farms, plantations and tropical greenery on Pulau Ubin (p.124).

Sightseeing: Witness the views of the mainland Singapore from the hilltops on Kusu Island (p.124).

Outdoor: Hike, bike or camp on peaceful Pulau Ubin (p.124), or check out the tranquil beaches on St John's Island (p.126).

Tours & Sightseeing

Taking a tour can be the best way to get your bearings and explore, no matter how long your stay. Just choose your mode of transport and away you go.

Tourism is one of Singapore's key service industries and while it's largely due to the Singapore Tourism Board's efforts that this is so, the country also recognises the need to keep growing the sector.

Most of the popular tours of the city are offered by a number of tour operators, but there are options too numerous to mention here – you can go on tarot reading tours, nature walks, chocolate trails and just about whatever you fancy. Many of the tour operators (see the table on p.139) will be more than happy to tell you all that they offer, or to tailor make a tour for you.

The Singapore Tourism Board (STB) visitors centres (p.21) are excellent resources: they'll give you information,

Junk Rider

Cruise around Singapore waters on a traditional Chinese junk and catch a glimpse of the past. The two and a half hour tour includes a stop at Kusu Island and costs $23 for adults and $11 for children. Several of the tour companies offer junk cruises, see Tour Operators on p.139 for contact details. One company worth checking out is SH Tours.

make bookings and sell you tickets, but most major hotels, travel agents and the tour operators listed on page 139 can help you with bookings too. STB also publishes The Official Guide & Map which lists individual operators, and their website (www. visitsingapore.com) is also useful.

Companies like City-Discovery.com (www.city-discovery. com/singapore) offer you a central online booking centre, which means you don't need to decide between the various operators, as they've done it for you. In general it's useful to try and book a tour two or three days in advance and you may be asked to pay a 50% deposit to secure your booking.

This section will provide you with plenty of inspiration and when you do go out, remember to dress comfortably with good, 'sensible' shoes for any walking that may be done. Hat, sunglasses and sunblock will be essential, especially on any boat or open-top bus rides. And don't forget your camera.

Boat Tours

Faber Tours
6377 9640

109 Mount Faber Rd, Telok Blangah   www.fabertours.com.sg

Faber Tours' Port Discovery Tour explores the southern tip of the island for a glimpse of Singapore's ports, Pasir Panjang Wharf, Pasir Panjang Terminal, Keppel Terminal, Tanjong Pagar Terminal, and Mount Faber. The tour includes a cable car ride and a pick-up service from hotels in the city. A three and a half hour tour, tickets cost $49 for adults and $39 for children. ⬛ HarbourFront, Map p.276 C3

Singapore DUCKtours

6338 6877

Various locations www.ducktours.com.sg

With their bright yellow amphibious craft, it's hard to miss the DUCK crew. They offer a combination city and harbour tour in a military craft that dates back to the Vietnam War. The 'Ducktainers' take you through historical landmarks around the Civic District before you splash into the water for views of the Merlion Park, the Esplanade and Clifford Pier. You'll board at the DUCKcounter at Suntec City Mall and tickets cost $33 for adults, $17 for children and $2 for children aged 1 to 2 years.

Singapore Explorer

6339 6833

Various locations www.singaporeexplorer.com.sg

Singapore Explorer offer tours by both bumboat and glass-top boat. Taking a bumboat along the Singapore River is an excellent way to get a feel for the city or if you prefer your sightseeing in air-conditioned comfort, you can take in the fabulous views in a glass top boat. The boats leave from Clarke Quay and Raffles Place MRT Jetty daily from 09:00 to 23:00.

Watertours Pte Ltd

6533 9811

HarbourFront Centre, Telok Blangah www.watertours.com.sg

Start or end your day of sightseeing sailing down the river on the Cheng Ho, a replica Chinese junk boat dating from the Ming Dynasty period. Boats depart daily at 10:30, 15:00 or 18:00 for the various routes, each one exploring different sites and islands. All cruises include light refreshments and/or high tea or dinner and prices start at $25 for adults and $12 for children. Cruises last around two hours. 🚇 HarbourFront, Map p.276 C3

Clockwise from top left: Esplanade Bridge and Suntec, Esplanade – Theatres on the Bay, The Merlion

Brewery Tours

TigerLIVE

6376 9339

St James Power Station, Telok Blangah   www.tigerlive.com.sg

Since Singapore is the home of Tiger beer, fans of the golden stuff make sure The Tiger Brewery Tour is on their itinerary. Tours will take you through the whole brewing process, ending with a few all-important tasting sessions. Open to visitors Monday to Friday (except Public Holidays). Tours take place daily – the first at 10:00 and the last at 18:00. Advance booking required. 🚇 HarbourFront, Map p.276 C3 **57**

Bus Tours

SH Tours

6734 9923

Various locations

www.asiatours.com.sg

The SIA Hop-On Bus is a special tourist bus service that offers a hop-on, hop-off service at designated stops around the city. You can buy a day pass from the driver and enjoy unlimited air-conditioned bus rides around the city's shopping, dining, cultural and entertainment areas. The Hop-On runs daily from 09:00 to 18:00 at 30 minute intervals. Day passes are free for Singapore Stopover Holidays passengers, $3 for SIA and SilkAir Passengers and $6 for other passengers.

Singapore DUCKtours

6338 6877

Various locations

www.ducktours.com.sg

Your topless option in Singapore, the HiPPOtour takes you around the city on an open-top double-decker. It has three types of tours, a city tour, a Sentosa tour which only takes you up to Sentosa and the heritage tour. The tours cost $23 for a one day pass and you can also buy a two-day unlimited Singapore Sightseeing Pass that includes and river cruise and their famous Red Lantern Tour for $13 for adults, $7 for children. You'll find a DUCKtours counter at Suntec City Mall.

Singapore Explorer
Various locations

6339 6833
www.singaporeexplorer.com.sg

Straight from the 1920s, the Singapore Trolley offers you a chance to amble through the colonial, cultural and art districts of Singapore at a gentler pace. The Trolley travels from the malls of Orchard Road to the colonial district and on to Clarke Quay with a narration of the sights you're passing. It takes about an hour to complete the 17 stop route and you can hop on and off as you please.

Sightseeing Tours

City in Transformation Tour
This covers the Financial District, Boat Quay, Chinese temples on Waterloo Street, a Hindu temple, a synagogue, a Catholic church and Arab Street. The three and a half hour tour costs $28 for adults and $14 for children. A number of tour operators offer this tour. See Tour Operators on p.139.

Round Island Tour
A full day tour that takes you to the outskirts of the city to places like the Haw Par Villa, Kranji War Memorial, Bright Hill

Temple and Johore Battery. Pick-ups from your hotel are from 08:30 and tickets cost from $74 for adults and $37 for children under 10. For companies offering this tour, see Tour Operators on p.139.

Shop & Eat

Combine the twin obsessions of all who live in Singapore. This tour takes you through some of Chinatown's most famous shops and eateries. Find some brilliant buys and sample a variety of delicacies and snacks. Tours cost around $45 for adults, $25 for children and last about three-and-a-half hours. Tour companies like Holiday Tours & Travel offer variations on this theme, for details see the Tour Operators table on p.139.

Transit Tour
Singapore Changi Airport   www.visitsingapore.com

If you're in transit in Singapore for at least five hours, check out this free two-hour sightseeing tour of the city. Register at the Singapore Visitors Centres at the Arrivals & Transit Halls at Changi Airport. Counters are open from 08:00 to 16:25 and seats are allocated on a first come first serve basis. If you hold a passport that requires a visa for Singapore, you will need one in order to do the tour. 🔲 Changi Airport, Map p.277 F2

CityCab   6542 5831
They'll collect you!   www.citycab.com.sg

On the Singapore Cabby Tour, trained drivers operate tours including a Round Island Tour, Singapore by Night Tour, Local Foods and Attractions Tour and Eastern and Western Heartland tours. You get to see the island in the comfort of a taxi with a a real-life taxi driver showing you the way. Call to book and your driver will pick you up from anywhere. Prices start from $105 per car for a three to six hour tour.

Helicopter Tours

ST Aerospace

Seletar Airport, Seletar

6481 0546
www.staero.aero

Up to four passengers and one pilot can take this 60 minute flight around Singapore. You'll get to see about two-thirds of the island, but won't be allowed to take any pictures as there are some concerns about national security. A flight costs $2,500

but if you want to fly on the weekend you'll have to pay a premium. To book a flight, call the office and have your passport details at hand. Map p.277 D1

Heritage Tours

Changi Tours

Created by the Changi Chapel & Museum, these two tours offer you insights into battle strategies and life during World War II. The Battlefield Tour covers historically important sites while the Changi WWII tour offers a glimpse of life as a prisoner of war. The Battlefield Tour costs $25 per adult, $20 per child, and the Changi WWII tour costs $40 per adult, $20 per child. For details companies who offer these tours see the Tour Operators table opposite.

Invasion Tour

Follow the footsteps of Japanese soldiers as they launched the invasion of Singapore during the World War II. Starting from the North, the four-hour tour covers the Japanese War Memorial, Kranji War Memorial, Bukit Chandu, Pasir Panjang and Labrador Park, and Alexander Barracks. Tickets cost $49. One of the companies that offers this tour is Malaysia and Singapore, for details see the Tour Operators table opposite

Peranakan Trail

Discover the history, culture and lifestyle of the Peranakan babas and nonyas. You'll be taken on a walk through a spice garden, see a fascinating display of Peranakan costume and jewellery, look at the rich architecture and enjoy some nonya delicacies. Tours start at 08:30 with a hotel pick-up and cost $39 for adults, $19.50 for children under 10. For details of tour companies see the Tour Operators table below.

Rags to Riches Tour With Trishaw Ride

This tour allows you to pretend to be an old-fashioned towkay (a Chinese tycoon) for the day. The tour starts at the Chinese Heritage Centre and takes in a traditional teahouse, a trishaw ride through Chinatown, and on to Boat Quay. This three-and-a-half hour tour costs $75 for adults, $37 for children under 10. You can book through www.city-discovery.com.

Tour Operators

Club Med Singapore	6830 0889	www.clubmed.com.sg
Faber Tours	6377 9640	www.fabertours.com.sg
Holiday Tours & Travel	6738 2622	na
Journeys	6325 1631	na
Malaysia & Singapore Travel Centre	6737 8877	na
RMG Tours	6220 1661	www.rmgtours.com
SH Tours	6734 9923	www.asiatours.com.sg
Siakson Coach Tours	6336 0288	na
Singapore DUCKtours	6338 6877	www.ducktours.com.sg
Singapore Explorer	6339 6833	www.singaporeexplorer.com.sg
Singapore River Cruise	6336 6111	www.rivercruise.com.sg
Watertours Pte Ltd	6533 9811	www.watertours.com.sg

Sports & Spas

Introduction

Prise yourself away from the fabulous malls and out-of-this-world restaurants of Singapore and you'll find a more active way to enrich your stay.

A break is the perfect time to try a new activity, re-visit a forgotten hobby or just relax. Despite the city-state's small size, there are many activities to be enjoyed. Take a glance at this chapter for more about how to make the most of your leisure time.

From chartering luxury motorcruisers to the more adventurous pursuits of waterskiing, wakeboarding and kayaking, there are a wide array of water-based pursuits to choose from. Take a look at p.144 for more on how to charter a sunset tour on a yacht or enjoy an afternoon anchored off the west coast whilst you indulge in a barbecue. Take advantage of the monsoon winds as you windsurf; plunge the depths of the ocean with an inspiring deep sea dive.

It is this natural world which provides an enthralling distraction from the hustle and bustle of the city. Get closer to the indigenous wildlife by camping in one of Singapore's parks, or fishing for baramundi and mangrove jack.

Unwind with a hike in a rainforest, where exotic birds such as parakeets and sunbirds flourish in their spectacular surroundings. See Outdoor Activities on page 148 for a guide to the best ways of spotting the indigenous flora and fauna through treetop walks and peaceful waterside trails. With its hectic city pace, taking time out to rejuvenate is very important to the inhabitants of Singapore. For such a small country, Singapore has an amazing number of golf courses (many of them superb, created by some of the world's best designers). Enjoy the sensation of teeing off in a tropical paradise (see p.154).

If you're a fan of spas you've also come to the right place. From meditation to massage, scrubs to steams, the treatments on offer will leave you feeling lighter, brighter and ready for more sight-seeing. Pools, waterfalls and lush gardens will ease away your cares, as you experience the benefits of Indian meditation, labyrinths and open-air rooftop gardens. Find out how sea water, mud, algae and sand can all offer therapeutic delights. Many have a local twist using Indian, Japanese and Chinese techniques and ingredients. Whatever your choice, Singapore won't disappoint.

Activity Finder

Watersports

Experience a different side of Singapore – from the water. Heading out to sea can be the best way to escape the heat and humidity.

Boat & Yacht Charters

Despite its often murky waters and busy shipping lanes, Singapore can be a fun place to hop on a boat and go for a trip; there is an abundance of activities available for those who love the sea. Quite a few outfits offer day trips, while some go on extended voyages. Day trips usually involve an early morning start and can include activities like kayaking, relaxing with a beer in a boom net, enjoying a barbecue, or, for the more adventurous, wakeboarding. The day usually ends with a quiet view of the sunset before heading back to shore. Also see Boat Tours on page 131.

Boats, Boats & Boats

6861 6965
Raffles Marina, Tuas
www.bbboats.com

Boats, Boats & Boats has two 48ft luxury motor cruisers with crew available for charter. Based out of the Raffles Marina, they offer day trips to the Southern Islands and Johore Straits. Overnight trips can also be arranged. A popular option is the Sunset BBQ, where the yacht anchors off the west coast for a sunset-and-grill session. You can bring your own food or arrange a barbecue package. Each yacht takes a maximum of 10 passengers. Map p.276 A2

Four Friends

6747 3105

Changi Sailing Club, Changi   www.schoonerfourfriends.com

The Four Friends is an attractive 60ft schooner skippered by the charismatic Warren Blake. Options include a day cruise, a sunset tour or an extended multi-day trip to explore far-away islands in Malaysia or further afield. The boat can sleep 12 in three cabins, four in the main deckhouse and the additional option of sleeping up on deck under the stars. Four Friends is equipped to support diving trips, and also has three sit-on-top kayaks and a 21ft motor launch. ▣ Pasir Ris, Map p.277 F2

Maxout Hydrosports

6869 2291

Raffles Marina, Tuas   www.maxouthydrosports.com

Maxout Hydrosports is located in the far west of Singapore, at Raffles Marina. They have three motor yachts for rent for day trips, mainly around the west of the island and the minimum rental period is six hours. Each boat can take a maximum of 12 people and a popular option is to do a combination rental with a yacht and a ski boat. Map p.276 A2

Wakeboarding & Waterskiing

Wakeboarding has caught on in the past few years and has eclipsed waterskiing in popularity – for the time being anyway. Operators offer lessons as well as boat and equipment rentals. Rates are usually hourly per boat (rather than per person) and generally include rental of life jackets and wakeboards or waterskis. Punggol, the Kallang River, and the East Coast Lagoon are regarded as the best locations, or try the unique Ski 360° (p.146). Prices range from $85 up to $120 per hour.

See Extreme Sports & Marketing (www.extreme.com.sg) and Ponggol Sea Sports (www.pssa.com.sg) for more details.

Ski 360°
1206A East Coast Parkway

6442 7318
www.ski360degree.com

Located near the East Coast Seafood Centre, Ski 360° opened in 2006 and is Singapore's first cableski park. It can accommodate eight wakeboarders or water skiers at a time, averaging 140-150 riders per day on weekends. Passes cost $40 for one hour on weekends or $30 on weekdays, with a 50% discount for a second hour. The fee includes rental of a life jacket, helmet and wakeboard or water skis. The park is lit at night, allowing enthusiasts to ride the waves until 22:00. Bedok, Map p.277 E3

Windsurfing

Singapore has two monsoon seasons a year, which means good winds for windsurfers. The north-east monsoon season from November to March is generally the best time to windsurf, although the south-west monsoon season from June to September comes a close second. Despite the monsoons, the winds in Singapore are not overly strong, so it's a good place for beginners to started. The main windsurfing spots are the waters off East Coast Park (p.83) and off Changi Beach (map p.277 F2). A short 45 minute ferry ride from the Tanah Merah Ferry Terminal, the Indonesian island of Bintan is also a popular destination. If you go, be sure to check out the Mana Mana Beach Club in Bintan (www.manamana.com), host of the Amslam windsurfing event held as part of the Asian Windsurfing Tour.

SAF Yacht Club

Pasta Fresca Sea Sports Centre

6449 1855

1212 East Coast Parkway, East Coast

The Pasta Fresca Sea Sports Centre hires out windsurfing equipment and has storage space for windsurfers with their own equipment. Windsurfing courses are offered throughout the week. Importantly, it also provides reliable and prompt rescue services. 🚇 Bedok, Map p.277 E3

SAF Yacht Club

6758 3032

Nr Woodlands Ind Est, Sembawang

www.safyc.org.sg

The Singapore Armed Forces Yacht Club offers a wide range of options for aspiring windsurfers. A basic windsurfing course costs $90 for non-members. Sailboards can be rented for $6 to $10 per hour. It also has two clubhouses and a sea sports centre. 🚇 Sembawang, Map p.277 D1

Outdoor Activities

Take advantage of Singapore's unique environment by hiking, kayaking or birdwatching. Fresh air awaits you, so pack your walking boots and camera.

Birdwatching

Singapore offers birdwatchers opportunities to see a huge variety of birds in a relatively small area. One day could easily comprise a morning in jungle, followed by a late afternoon outing to a wetland area. Singapore has recorded over 350 species sightings, of which about 150 are resident birds. Species include the red-crowned barbet, chestnut-bellied malkoha, long-tailed parakeet and copper-throated sunbird. Recommended sites are Bukit Timah Nature Reserve (p.93), one of the last remaining patches of primary forest, and the MacRitchie Reservoir Park (p.94). Jurong BirdPark (below) also has an impressive variety of birdlife in a relatively compact area.

Jurong BirdPark

2 Jurong Hill, Jurong

6265 0022
www.birdpark.com.sg

A dizzying array of over 9,000 birds from 600 species inhabits this 20 hectare park and its four aviaries. Regular bird shows are held, demonstrating the birds' unique characteristics. Special attractions include the Lory Loft, Pelican Cove, Penguin Parade and the World of Darkness. The park is great for families and kids, but also worthwhile for serious bird enthusiasts. 🚇 Boon Lay, Map p.276 B3

Jurong BirdPark

Camping

Singapore's hot and humid climate (with the occasional torrential downpour) can make sleeping outdoors slightly uncomfortable, although setting up camp near the ocean offers a refreshing break from the heat. In addition, camping here is not exactly a true wilderness experience, as you'll most likely be pitching a tent on a manicured lawn under some trees, and it is not encouraged as a form of backpackers' accommodation. But if you're set on experiencing life outdoors, several of Singapore's parks are good places to head to, and details can be found on the National Parks website at www.nparks.gov.sg. While there are no camping fees, permits are required for weekdays and, conveniently, park rangers will come by your tent to issue these, (for a maximum of three consecutive nights). Further afield, Pulau Ubin (below) is a wilder camping destination just a short boat trip away.

Pulau Ubin
North east of Singapore

6542 4108
www.npark.gov.sg

A $2 bumboat ride from Changi Point Ferry Terminal will get you to Pulau Ubin, a large island off the north east coast of Singapore. The developed parts of Pulau Ubin are said to be like a trip back to the Singapore of the 1960s, with kampong-style life still eking out a small existence. There are a number of grocery stores where you can pick up food and any supplies you might have forgotten. Tents can be pitched at the beach campsites of Noordin, Mamam or Jelutong, all of which have toilet facilities, although only Jelutong has designated fire pits. No permits are required. Map p.277 F1

Fishing

Singapore has many opportunities for fishing, from shore casting and stocked fish ponds to charters in coastal waters and deep sea fishing. The fish ponds dotted around the island are usually stocked with barramundi, mangrove jack, golden pomfret and snapper. Shore casting is possible along Singapore's rivers, coastline and at designated areas in most reservoirs. Fishing charters can be arranged from most marinas. The Sport Fishing Association (Singapore) has a website at www.sfas.net and is a good start for information on how and where to fish in Singapore.

Ah Bee Charter   9616 8895
Marina Country Club, Punggol

Veteran fisherman Ah Bee will take you and up to four other anglers for day charter trips into the coastal waters around Changi. The trip lasts from 07:00-16:30 and costs $350, which does not include food, bait or tackle, although water and ice are provided. With a focus on bottom-fishing, you're likely to catch grouper, snapper and barramundi. 🚇 Punggol, Map p.277 E2

Anglers Hut   6298 1015
10 Bussorah St, Arab Street & Kampong Glam

Anglers Hut is a full service tackle shop that also offers fishing charters. In addition to day trips in Singapore waters, extended trips to Malaysia can be arranged. An evening van ride will take you up to Rompin in Pahang province in three and a half hours, where you'll stay overnight in a hotel. In the morning the boat heads for the open water where you'll get a chance to do battle with sailfish that can weigh in at over 30kg! Most trips give two days on the water. Contact the Anglers Hut for details on costs and the next scheduled trip. 🚌 Bugis, Map p.285 E4 ▮

Night Anglers
9154 0722
SAF Yacht Club, Changi

Based out of the SAF Yacht Club, Night Anglers provides day and night charter trips in the waters around Tanah Merah and the Johor shore. Day trips cost $350 and run from 08:30-18:00, while night trips cost $390 and last from 19:30-07:00. The price of the trip includes ice, water and hot drinks, but not food, bait or tackle. Trips can accommodate up to six anglers and the boat has a toilet and a proper wheelhouse for shelter. Daylight will see you catching smaller fish, like diamond trevally. At night you'll be reeling in snapper, grouper, stingray and barracuda. 🚌 Pasir Ris, Map p.277 F2

Hiking

The central and northern parts of Singapore are a haven for hikers. Head to Bishan Park (p.93), Bukit Timah Nature Reserve (p.93) and the MacRitchie Reservoir (p.94) to satisfy your yearning for the outdoors. Bukit Timah is home to hundreds of species of flowering plants and animals, while the MacRitchie offers a 250 metre Treetop Walk. Keep your eyes open and you're likely to spot monkeys, lizards and birds. When exploring, be sure to bring ample water, bug spray and a mobile phone. For more information call the National Parks Board at 6471 7808 or check out www.nparks.gov.sg.

Kayaking

Kayaking in Singapore takes place in two environments: out on the ocean, or in the inland reservoirs. Popular trips include Pulau Ubin, the Southern Islands, Seletar Island or just paddling along the coast. Kayaking in the reservoirs is supposed to be limited to organised groups and public rental from appointed clubs that run a centre at the reservoirs. You can kayak in most of the reservoirs in Singapore, including MacRitchie, Bedok, Upper and Lower Seletar and Pandan.

Paddle Lodge   6258 0057
MacRitchie Reservoir, Central Singapore

The Paddle Lodge at the far eastern end of MacRitchie Reservoir is the Singapore Canoe Federation's main facility. You can rent two types of kayaks; sit-on-top kayaks, $10 per hour, are available to anyone and come in one or two-seater versions. Conventional kayaks (where you sit with your legs on the inside) are available at $15 per hour, but only to paddlers with a one star certification. For more details log on to www.scf.org.sg/Facilities/PLDetails.html. ▣ Braddell, Map p.277 D2

People's Association Sea Sports Club   6340 5335
Various locations   www.seasports.org.sg

The People's Association runs a number of paddle centres where you can rent kayaks, get instruction and try out sea kayaking. Locations are at Changi (6545 1140), East Coast (6444 0409), Kallang (6296 6883) and Pasir Ris (6582 4796). Paddlezinc (6340 5335) at the Bedok Reservoir gives you the option of slightly calmer water in pleasant surroundings.

Golf

Tee off at some of the world's finest greens; you'll find an impressive choice, from smaller clubs used by expats to the flashiest competition courses.

For such a small country, Singapore has a great number of golf courses. Many have been designed by prestigious names and had multi-million dollar renovations, and it shows in the quality of the experience. Top end courses can be found at the Laguna Golf Club (opposite) and Sentosa Golf Club (p.156), and most courses have facilities such as clubhouses, restaurants and lounges. You will usually have to be a member or a member's guest, but some clubs allow walk-ons during the week.

Changi Golf Club   6545 5133
20 Netheravon Rd, Changi

The Changi Golf Club is a hilly nine hole, par 34 course. A second set of tee-boxes allow for your second round to have a different feel from the first. It's open to walk-on golfers on weekdays, but weekends are reserved for members and guests. There is a small chipping area, but no driving range. 🚇 Pasir Ris, Map p.277 F2

Green Fairways   6468 7233
60 Fairways Drive, Bukit Timah

Another nine-hole course that is primarily an option if you want to get in a few holes but haven't secured a booking elsewhere. You can walk on at any time and get a tee time fairly quickly. The course is a par 33 and plays 1,660m long. Costs are $42 for nine holes during the week and $52 on the weekend. 🔲 Bukit Batok, Map p.276 C2

Keppel Club
6375 5528
10 Bukit Chermin Rd, Telok Blangah   www.keppelclub.com.sg

Set at the southern tip of Singapore, this golf course offers 5,987m of undulating terrain. The par 72 course has numerous bunkers and hazards to challenge golfers of all levels. There is a two-level driving range where resident golf pros provide lessons for beginners and seasoned golfers alike. You will need to have an official handicap before playing and tests can be arranged. 🔲 HarbourFront, Map p.278 C3 🔲

Laguna National Golf & Country Club
6542 6888
11 Laguna Golf Green, Tanah Merah   www.lagunagolf.com.sg

The two par 72, 18 hole courses at this club offer distinctly different golfing experiences. The Masters Course is designed in the old Scottish tradition of pronounced fairway mounds and water features. The Classic Course has more of an American feel to it, with large bunkers and a premium on the short game. There is also a three tier driving range, and an area for honing your short game. 🔲 Tanah Merah, Map p.277 E3

Orchid Country Club
6750 2111
1 Orchid Club Rd, Yishun   www.orchidclub.com

Three distinct nine-hole courses make up the 27 hole international championship course at the Orchid Country

Club. The three courses – Aranda (par 36, 3,037m), Vanda (par 36, 3,051m) and Dendro (par 37, 3,262m) – are named after orchids. At 590m, the Dendro course's third hole is one of Singapore's longest par fives. The 160 bay driving range, with a computerised automatic lower deck, is considered one of the best in the city. There's also a four-hole practice course with two par fours and two par threes. ▣ Khatib, Map p.277 D1

Raffles Country Club

6861 7655

Ayer Rajah Expressway, Tuas

www.rcc.org.sg

This club has two par 72, 18 hole courses designed by Robert Trent Jones Junior. The Lake Course has 5,819m of rolling fairways set alongside the Tengeh Reservoir. The 6,081m Palm Course is a challenging mix of bunkers and water hazards, and hosted the Asia PGA Championships in 1997 and 1998. There's a handicap requirement and Saturday afternoons are reserved for members only. Map p.276 A2

Seletar Base Golf Course

6481 4745

244 Oxford St, Seletar

www.seletarbaseclub.org.sg

This course was built in 1930 as a golf club for the British Air Force. It has since changed hands and is now a public nine-hole course. There is also a chip-and-putt course for practicing your short game and a driving range. ▣ Khatib, Map p.277 D1

Sentosa Golf Club

6275 0090

Bukit Manis Rd, Sentosa

www.sentosagolf.com

One of Singapore's most exclusive and magnificent golfing venues, Sentosa's two 18 hole championship courses offer challenging holes among rolling hills at the eastern end of the island with stunning views of Singapore Harbour and the South China Sea. The Serapong course was voted one of the top five in Asia by Asian Golf Monthly. The club also has a driving range and a golf academy. 🚇 HarbourFront, Map p.299 D3 **3**

Singapore Island Country Club
Central Singapore

6459 2222
www.sicc.org.sg

Braddell, Map p.277 D2

The SICC boasts four 18 hole courses set along the MacRitchie and Peirce Reservoirs and two separate clubhouses. The Bukit Course and New Course, both par 72, have limited access for non-members – see the website for details. The Island Course is hilly with views of the reservoir, while the Sime Course is in a treed, park-like setting. Both are par 71. There is also a driving range and a nine-hole executive course. 🚇 Braddell, Map p.277 D2

Spas

Residents of Singapore take relaxation seriously, so where better to unwind and pamper yourself with some truly terrific treatments?

Everyone in Singapore is interested in taking care of themselves and looking their best and there is a strong Asian influence in many of the services offered, with Indian, Japanese and Chinese cultures leaving their mark on massage, yoga, meditation and more. There has been a huge increase in the number of health spas in recent years and you'll find facilities ranging from the most modern and cutting-edge to the more traditional, and there's no shortage of soothing ways to help you de-stress and walk out feeling rejuvenated and revitalised.

You'll find a good mix of Asian-inspired spas and those with more of a European influence here, and despite spas being perceived as mainly for women, many also offer treatments for men as well as couples' packages. Now that's quality time! Wherever your inner peace lies, you're sure to find it in Singapore.

Amrita Spa
Various locations

6336 4477
www.amritaspa.com

The Amrita Spa has branches at the Raffles Hotel, Raffles the Plaza (p.45) and Swissotel Merchant Court (6239 1780). The Raffles Hotel spa is exclusively for hotel guests, but the other two take walk-in customers. The spas offer a full range of treatments and special therapies including treatments for couples, golfers, jet lagged travellers and men's Kur and Sundari Ayurvedic spa rituals.

Andana Spa

6836 9988
The Paragon, Orchard　　　　www.andanaspa.com

Set on the top floor of The Paragon shopping centre, Andana – which is Sanskrit for paradise – has a full range of spa treatments to bring you relaxation and a renewed sense of mind and spirit. The deluxe spa package includes a 45 minute massage, unlimited food and beverages from their menu and the use of their pools, movie lounges and private rooms. 🚇 Orchard, Map p.282 C3 **4**

The Asian Spa

6877 8183
The Fullerton, Riverside　　　www.cosmoprof.com.sg

Set in the unique Fullerton Hotel, The Asian Spa sprawls over 20,000 square feet complete with rooftop pool. Signature services include hot stones therapy, aroma body massage and Javanese heritage treatments. Your skin will also feel clean and radiant after a body brushing using Dead Sea salts and black mud. 🚇 Raffles Place, Map p.296 C1 **5**

Aspara Spa

6879 2688
Various locations　　　　　　www.aspara.com.sg

The Aspara offers fragrant herbal baths, stress-releasing massages or a Tahitian body scrub to do wonders for your sense of wellbeing. And if you've been there, indulged in that,

they also do a Javanese lulur, which is a seaweed body wrap. Aspara has three branches, one at the Amara Hotel at Tanjong Pagar, another with a serene tropical garden at the Goodwood Hotel just off Orchard Road (6732 3933) and a recently opened Garden Spa at the Hollandse Club (6461 1146).

Benjaphan Thai Herbal Spa   6469 7622
559 Bukit Timah Rd, Bukit Timah   www.benjaphan.com

The Benjaphan Thai Herbal Spa in King's Arcade is great for an authentic Thai spa experience. There is lots of greenery and natural light, so you almost feel like you're getting your dose of indulgence in the great outdoors. Their signature treatments include Thai herbal steam therapy and a herbal compress treatment. 🚇 Newton, Map p.276 C3

Earth Sanctuary   6324 7933
86 Club St, Chinatown   www.earthsanctuary.com.sg

The Earth Sanctuary Spa offers holistic therapies in a rustic and intimate shophouse on Club Street. The diverse menu includes elements of Australian Aboriginal treatments, as well as Hawaiian, Javanese and Balinese therapies. A full range of massages, wraps, scrubs, baths and skin services are available, alongside a line of Earth Sanctuary private label products. 🚇 Chinatown, Map p.296 A3 **6**

Eucalyptus Day Spa   6324 1338
43A Craig Rd, Tanjong Pagar   www.eucalyptus.com.sg

This day spa, located in a 100 year old shophouse near Chinatown, offers therapies based on Eastern remedies (and

Top: Amrita Spa. Bottom: The Asian Spa

one or two from the modern-day West). You can relax in the private treatment rooms or the open-air rooftop garden while you are pampered. There are more than 10 different kinds of massages, plus Ayurvedic therapies, body scrubs and a treatment for everything from your head down to your feet. 🔲 Outram Park, Map p295 B4 **7**

Qi Mantra

6221 5691

83A Club St, Chinatown

www.qimantra.com

For a modern take on Chinese acupressure, head to Qi Mantra in Chinatown. They've taken traditional treatments and ingredients and blended them into therapies that match the modern decor of their spa. Try the 'general health blast', 'herbal punch' or even the 'gingerific blast' to work out the knots in your back, shoulders and neck. 🔲 Chinatown, Map p.296 A3 **8**

Renewal Day Spa

6738 0988

302 Orchard Rd, Orchard

www.renewal.com.sg

The decor may be that of the rustic Provencal countryside, but the spa menu at Renewal Day Spa is a blend of East, West and the latest techniques and technologies. This tranquil retreat in the Tong Building, just off bustling Orchard Road, is a great place to unwind. Hydrotherapy, body wraps and scrubs and a range of massages are all on offer. 🔲 Orchard, Map p.282 C3 **9**

The Retreat

6738 0080

Various locations

www.theretreat.com.sg

The Retreat specialises in Thalasso treatments, which involve the use of nutrient rich sea water, mud, algae and sand to stimulate the body. You can opt for the ground level treatment suites with lush garden surroundings, or go up to the suites on the eighth and ninth floors for spectacular sea views and rooftop showers. There are three branches of The Retreat: at Grand Hyatt (6416 7156), Marriott Hotel (6831 4526) and its flagship spa at Changi Village Hotel (6738 0080).

Spa Botanica
6371 1318
2 Bukit Manis Rd, Sentosa   www.spabotanica.com

The award-winning Spa Botanica at The Sentosa Resort & Spa is designed to make you forget the stress of urban life in its beautiful setting. Pools, waterfalls and lush gardens help you to relax and get the most out of your treatments and guests are encouraged to take a few minutes to walk the labyrinth to clear their minds before their spa sessions. Methods used here focus on natural ingredients to cleanse and revitalise and signature treatments include the 'galaxy steam bath', 'tropical glow' and 'Singapore flower ritual'. ◪ HarbourFront, Map p.299 D3 🔟

Vipassana International
9011 9432
St. John's Island, Southern Islands   www.sg.dhamma.org

Not a spa but a retreat, Vipassana International offers ten-day courses on St John's Island, 6.5km south of Singapore, in the Indian meditation technique of Vipassana, that strives for total liberation and enlightenment. Each day's schedule runs from the 04:00 wake-up bell to lights out at 21:00. The course is free – the organisation survives solely on the donations of past participants. For details of what is involved and how to get there, log on to their website. Map p.277 D4

Shopping

Shopping Singapore

If your therapy is of the retail variety, you're in the right place. With shiny new malls alongside traditional ethnic areas, there's shopping for everyone.

Singaporeans love a good bargain, and the retail landscape has been engineered to pander to that. There's always one sale or another taking place – pre and post Christmas, pre Chinese New Year, annual sales, seasonal sales... the list goes on. But the major shopathon penned in every true shopper's diary is the Great Singapore Sale (www.greatsingaporesale. com.sg) – the single most important annual shopping event. It takes place over two months, usually from May to July, during which virtually every department store, small retailer and even spas and car workshops slash their prices. The sale is so eagerly awaited by everyone on the island that on the first day, it's not uncommon for Singaporeans to take the day off work to be there long before the doors to their favourite store open, in eager anticipation of the bargains within.

Orchard Road (p.170) has the biggest concentration of malls. Here, from 11:00 to 21:30 every day (bar two days over Chinese New Year when most shops and restaurants close), you can browse through racks of international couture labels and high street brands in glitzy malls like Ngee Ann City (p.174) and Centrepoint (p.172). Seasoned shoppers then take a break at Starbucks for a latte, before continuing the quest for the latest plasma screen television or perhaps a diamond ring.

For those with a more adventurous shopping spirit, interesting finds may be discovered in areas like Holland Village, Chinatown, Little India and Arab Street (see next page), where you can pick up knick knacks, spices and even cutting edge fashion. In the past few years, young designers and edgy clothing stores have set up shop here, livening up the retail landscape with interesting alternatives to the mass market labels.

While big name international brand clothes tend to cost about 10% more in Singapore, there are enough local and regional brands of comparable quality and in the latest styles to satisfy your quest for fashion. Electronic goods here are among the cheapest in Asia and the latest models are generally released here at about the same time as the rest of the world. Computers and cameras (p.185) can cost 20 to 30% less than elsewhere – you just have to be prepared to shop around for the best price, and, of course, be ready to bargain.

In this chapter you'll find all of Singapore's hotspots (p.168) where you are guaranteed to flex the plastic, the best malls (p.172), and some insider tips to guarantee you head for the right place for the best buys in Singapore (p.184).

Tax & Duty Free

A 5% goods and services tax (GST) covers almost all goods and services. This charge is shown on price tags in chains and department stores, but at smaller shops you should check whether GST is included before you bargain. And if you're buying something big, ask about getting a rebate when you leave Singapore before you buy.

Hotspots

Leave the air conditioning behind and explore areas that haven't succumbed to the big brands and chain stores.

Arab Street

Kampong Glam

Arab Street is for textiles and fabrics. The entire street is filled with retailers and wholesalers who bring European fabrics in to Singapore and many local fashion designers source their fabrics here. For more on tailors, see p.187.

Wander down the side streets and you will be surprised by the interesting finds you make. Among the stores selling furniture and art there's a vintage shop with fashion and furniture fittings from the 60s and 70s on Bussorah Street. Wander down sleepy Haji Lane and you'll find artist workshops, stores selling fashion designed by art school students and a shop that sells chandeliers that the owners fashion themselves. 🚇 Bugis, Map p.285 E4 🚊

Chinatown

The central streets of Chinatown are packed with stalls selling all sorts of Chinese trinkets, ceramics and kitchenware. Chinese tourists shop for sweet red bak kwa, or barbecued pork – try the Bee Cheng Hiang brand – and every kind of weird and wonderful foods from pungent mushrooms to frogs, red crabs, flavoursome teas and medicinal cure-alls. The Tanjong Pagar market is especially good for fresh fruit, vegetables and flowers. On South Bridge Road are attractive but expensive antique shops. 🚇 Chinatown, Map p.295 F3 **2**

Holland Village

Singapore's 'bohemian enclave', Holland Village is a microcosm of life here. It's a curious mix of old and new, although the area is slowly becoming gentrified. Shops and restaurants occupy old two-storey shophouses and the buildings themselves are worth a look.

Popular with younger Singaporeans and expatriates, it is dominated by, and often visited solely for, its eateries and wine bars. In the last few years though, the area has also evolved into a bit of a shopping zone with some specialist shops to cater for the arty crowd. Antipodean at Lorong Mambong stocks Australian designers, accessories made by local designers as well as jeans from Paper Denim & Cloth. Galerie Cho Lon has an eclectic mix of Asian and European antiques and houseware and a small selection of art and books. 🚇 Buona Vista, Map p.278 B2 **3**

Little India

Walk down Little India's streets signposted in Tamil, Hindi and Bengali and shop for colourful saris, spices and Indian Barbie dolls – it's all here in colourful abundance. While it can be chaotic at times, it's also one of the more authentic experiences an outsider can enjoy in what can be a rather 'Asia-lite' Singapore. Like a real Indian city, what keeps this area so vibrant is the population it serves. On Sundays you'll experience Little India at its finest. 🚇 Little India, Map p.284 C3 **4**

Orchard Road

The Champs Elysees of Singapore, Orchard Road rivals all the other areas in terms of sheer volume, quality, and choice. Technically the area extends beyond Orchard Road: the shopping actually begins at Tanglin Road and extends up Orchard Road with a detour to Scotts Road where Far East Plaza (p.172), the Hyatt Hotel, Pacific Plaza (p.175) and DFS Galleria are. It continues all the way up Somerset Road to the Dhoby Ghaut area near Hotel Meridien. Walking from one end to another would take you about 40 minutes if you weren't side tracked by shops and food outlets along the way.

If you're looking for the big brand names and the latest fashion trends, you'll be spoilt for choice here, no matter what your budget is. A T-shirt can range from $5 to $5,000 along this shopping belt where budget shops sit next door to swish boutiques and customers range from window shoppers to big spenders.

🚇 Orchard, Map p.282 C3 **5**

Discussions of Budget

Bargaining is a bit of a sport in Singapore. While prices are fixed in the bigger stores, you can try for a discount at the smaller stores – even the ones along Orchard Road. Many will offer at least 10% off if you ask. Electronics sold at non chain stores are all open to bargaining. Shops in the ethnic and suburban areas in Singapore (especially if they're not air conditioned and their goods aren't price tagged) are also open to negotiation, so practise your best smile to get the best price.

The heat and humidity combined with the fight for prime space means Singapore is bursting with amazing air-conditioned shopping malls.

Centrepoint

6737 9000

176 Orchard Rd, Orchard

www.centrepoint.com.sg

This grand dame of Orchard Road malls has seen many renovations and upgrades over the years. It's the home of Robinson's (p.183), Singapore's oldest and most venerable department store. Centrepoint also houses the city's largest Marks & Spencer store carrying a limited selection of clothing, shoes, household items, food and lingerie.

The mall has a popular 'food street' in the basement offering a range of cuisines. You'll also find electronics and camera shops, CD shops, a pharmacy, shoe shops and a Cold Storage down here. You can book tickets for various arts shows at the information desk on the first floor and there's a parking complex at the back of the mall. 🚇 Somerset, Map p.283 E4 **6**

Far East Plaza

6734 6837

14 Scotts Rd, Orchard

www.fareast-plaza.com

A must for bargain hunters, Far East Plaza on Scotts Road boasts over 800 stores and eating places. Despite the hodge podge of businesses, it is becoming a hotbed of local design and experimental retail concepts. Far East Plaza is also home to Johnny Two Thumbs, Singapore's best-known and longest surviving tattoo parlour. 🚇 Orchard, Map p.282 B2 **7**

Forum The Shopping Mall

6732 2469

Nr Tanglin Centre, Orchard

About a 10 minute walk from Orchard MRT station, this shopping mall specialises in stuff for kids. Toys R Us is the anchor tenant here and the many fashion outlets for children include Guess Kids, Esprit Kids, Benetton Kids and Kids 21. To keep your energy up there's the city's only California Pizza Kitchen, a Coffee Bean & Tea Leaf, a conveyor-belt sushi place and a 24 hour McDonald's here. 🚇 Orchard, Map p.282 A2 **8**

The Heeren

6733 4725

260 Orchard Rd, Orchard

www.heeren.com.sg

Here's where you'll find HMV, the largest music superstore in south-east Asia. The first three floors of this mall offer big names in sports, streets and fashion. On levels four and five is Annex, which has everything from street and vintage fashion to accessories, quirky toys and comics.

The restaurants on the fifth level sell really good Asian food and for casual dining there's Movenpick's Marche in the basement or Balcony Bar, a two-storey bar with a rooftop mini Jacuzzi and sofas. While there is no adjoining parking lot, you can park at Cairnhill Place, accessible from Cairnhill Road or at The Paragon shopping centre. 🚇 Somerset, Map p.283 D4 **9**

Holland Village Shopping Centre

6468 5334

211 Holland Ave, Holland Village

This eclectic expat favourite is about 25 years old and its idiosyncrasies (the escalators only go up, for instance) only add to its charm. Shops here carry popular Balinese teak and Asian style furniture pieces Cafe 211 on the top floor is a charming deli with a rooftop seating area where you can refuel. ⬛ Buona Vista, Map p.278 B2 **10**

Marina Square

6339 8787
6 Raffles Blvd,Colonial District   www.marinasquare.com.sg

This 700,000 square foot space is divided into eight zones including food and restaurants, fashion, hobby, art and living. The walkways are wide and the high ceilings make it all feel light and spacious.

Giant takes up almost a third of the second floor so you can do all your grocery shopping here. Once that's out of the way you can start having fun at the mall's 20 bag and shoe shops, 36 men and women's fashion stores and 53 restaurants and food outlets. Marina Square is easily accessed from Suntec City and is seamlessly linked to Citylink Mall, Millenia Walk and the Esplanade theatres. ⬛ City Hall, Map p.291 E4 **11**

Ngee Ann City

6733 0337
391 Orchard Rd, Orchard   www.ngeeanncity.com.sg

Easily the largest mall on Orchard Road, Ngee Ann City is also called Takashimaya (p.183) by locals after its anchor tenant. Here, you'll find high-end designer stores, fastfood outlets, a hardware store, mobile phone centres and Kinokuniya (p.184), the largest bookshop in Singapore. It's probably the best place to avoid a heavy downpour, or if you need to pick up a variety of things under one roof. Ngee Ann City hosts a variety of high street labels and the city's only Hugo Boss store is here too, along with Celine, Gucci, Chanel, Louis

Vuitton, Fendi, and most other top designer brands. The basement food court is a great place to sample reasonably priced and tasty local food. Parking is ample (enter by Orchard Turn). 🚇 Orchard, Map p.282 C4 **12**

Pacific Plaza
6733 5655

9 Scotts Rd, Orchard

Although smaller than most Orchard Road malls, Pacific Plaza is one of the trendiest. That CD Shop is a fabulous place to explore new music and the Adidas concept store is popular with fashionistas. It also houses some of Australia's most popular surfwear lines with Stussy, Billabong, Rip Curl and Quiksilver represented. If you're into vintage you'll enjoy going through the racks at The Vintage Place. 🚇 Orchard, Map p.282 B2 **13**

The Paragon
6738 5535

290 Orchard Rd, Orchard

The Paragon is a haven for fashionistas with its diverse mix of international brands – Gucci, Valentino, Jean Paul Gaultier, Burberry and Versace – and edgier, newer labels. Here you'll find Potion, a local fashion label as well as edgy street fashion labels like G-Star, Miss Sixty and Diesel. The anchor tenant is homegrown department store Metro which takes up three floors at one end of the mall. There's also a Marks & Spencer.

But perhaps one of the things this mall is best known for is its outstanding washrooms complete with large sofas. The mall's multi-storey car park is accessible by Bideford Road just off Orchard Road. 🚇 Orchard, Map p.282 C3 **14**

Park Mall

6339 8229

9 Penang Rd, Orchard

If you're mad about furniture and interiors, this is the place to come to for inspiration. There are small food places that serve local fare in the basement, as well as a Watson's 'personal care' store. Heng Nam Nam is a dressmaker whose clientele consists mainly of 'ladies who lunch'. Situated across from Plaza Singapura, parking is fairly easy with the entrance to the mall accessible from Penang Road. 🚇 Dhoby Ghaut, Map p.289 F1 **15**

People's Park Complex

6535 9533

1 Park Rd, Chinatown

Hailed as a masterpiece of 1970s experimental architecture from the Japanese Metabolist Movement, People's Park Complex is said to represent the significant trends that have prevailed in Singapore over the last four decades. In shopping terms, it's a condensed version of a Chinese downtown and is great for bargains of all sorts, with extensive ranges of electronic goods, luggage, textiles, bargain-priced clothes and cosmetics, and even antiques. 🚇 Chinatown, Map p.295 F2 **16**

Plaza Singapura

6332 9298

68 Orchard Rd, Orchard

One of the last malls on the Orchard Road stretch, Plaza Singapura places the emphasis on fashion, entertainment and food for families and young adults. Its retail outlets are spread over nine themed floors and Golden Village Plaza, or the GV Plaza as it's known, is a popular cineplex with seven cinemas. 🚇 Somerset, Map p.283 F4 **17**

Left: Raffles City Shopping Centre, Right: VivoCity

Raffles City Shopping Centre

6338 7766

252 North Bridge Rd, Colonial District   www.rafflescity.com

Designed by renowned architect IM Pei, this shopping mall is attached to the Swissotel, The Stamford, and Raffles and The Plaza hotels. The Raffles City Convention Centre and shopping complexes are in the immediate area so it's a great spot to explore if you're staying or working nearby.

The supermarket Marketplace and Robinson's department store (p.183) are the main tenants here alongside UK and US high street labels. There are also electronics stores, sports shops, kids' fashion, toys and a variety of restaurants. Cedele serves some of the best sandwiches in town and The Soup Spoon is constantly packed.

All the major local banks have ATMs in the basement, and parking is ample. Parking charges are $2 for the first hour and $1 for every 30 minutes thereafter from Mondays to Saturdays. After 18:00, charges drop to $2. 🚇 City Hall, Map p.290 C3 **18**

Suntec City Mall
6825 2667
3 Temasek Blvd, Suntec
www.sunteccity.com.sg

Suntec City Mall consists of about 270 stores in 888,000 feng shui-ed square feet of shopping, and taking pride of place in the middle is the Fountain of Wealth (p.59). It is designed to attract prosperity and locals visit this 'monument' daily to try to get their share of good luck. The mall has been divided into various zones. You'll find shops for golf, office and fashion wear, luggage, furniture, books, electronics, bridal shops, jewellery, children's fashions, and even hearing aids in this vast complex.

The Eng Wah Cineplex is a hidden gem, with comfortable seats, great service, gentle air conditioning that won't freeze you to death and, best of all, it's always easy to get a seat here.

When parking at Suntec City, make a note of where your car is. In fact, it might be good to write down exactly which zone you're in (they're named after animals) and which lot number you've parked in. 🚇 City Hall, Map p.291 E2 **19**

Tanglin Mall
6736 4922
163 Tanglin Rd, Tanglin
www.tanglinmall.com.sg

Just a five minute walk away from Tanglin Shopping Centre, the more 'suburban' Tanglin Mall caters to the residents who live nearby. There's a World of Sports outlet, That CD shop, a large British India store that stocks clothes and houseware, a Birkenstocks shop, tailor, Barang Barang and numerous fashion outlets. 🖪 Orchard, Map p.281 E3 **20**

Tanglin Shopping Centre

6737 0849

19 Tanglin Rd, Tanglin

A short walk from frenzied Orchard Road, Tanglin Shopping Centre is comparatively mellow and laidback. Chock-a-block with Chinese and Tibetan antiques, Persian carpets, tapestries and curio shops it's like a mini-UN of artefacts. Tanglin Shopping Centre is known for its numerous Japanese restaurants on the fourth floor. Tambuah Mas, probably Singapore's oldest Indonesian restaurant, has been here for over 20 years and is a firm favourite. 🖪 Orchard, Map p.281 F2 **21**

VivoCity

6377 6860

HarbourFront Centre, Telok Blangah   www.vivocity.com.sg

Designed by Toyo Ito, a well-renowned Japanese architect, VivoCity mall open in late 2006 and zoomed into the record books as the largest mall in Singapore, at a whopping 1.04 million square feet. There's retail space, a fleet of outdoor restaurants along the harbourside promenade, a rooftop sky park and ampitheatre, a Cineplex boasting 2,293 seats and an open-air playground. In short, VivoCity is the big daddy of shopping malls – with the retail-hungry crowds to match. There are two food courts for refueling – Food Republic and Kopitiam/Banquet, and on the basement level you'll find a kingdom of fastfood outlets.

Then, there's the shops. VivoCity houses Singapore's first Gap store, its only stand-alone Principles boutique and Ted Baker store, as well as sportswear shops including Nike and Puma. Alternatively, if you're not into shopping, Eu Yan Sang, the chinese medicine empire, has a gorgeous concept store called Red White & Pure, incorporating a spa and 70 seat dining area. This mall is an airy and futuristic architectural wonder. ◨ HarbourFront, Map p.298 C1 **22**

Wisma Atria Shopping Centre

623 2103

435 Orchard Rd, Orchard

www.wismaonline.com

Refurbished in 2006, the mall is covered in blue glass and is something of a landmark on Singapore's busiest shopping strip. It houses over 100 trendy mid to high end fashion boutiques and other lifestyle stores on its five floors. Each floor has its unique identity; the basement, for example, is famous for its floor to ceiling aquarium. As the floors progress upwards, the stores become higher end with upmarket international brands. Level four has a food court where you can choose from self service stalls or have food served to you from one of the pushcarts that do the rounds.

On the ground floor you can buy tickets to performances at the ticketing counter and tourists can do GST refunds. At the nearby concierge counter you can book city tours, make flight reservations and even request for a limousine to pick you up.

The mall is linked to Orchard MRT station and is also linked by an underground passage to Lucky Plaza and Ngee Ann City. ◨ Orchard, Map p.282 B3 **23**

Department Stores

Before the malls arrived, Singapore's department stores were the backbone of shopping culture and they still have plenty to offer today.

Isetan

6733 1111

Shaw House, Orchard

www.isetan.com.sg

The Japanese department store Isetan has four stores in Singapore: its flagship store at Shaw House on the corner of Scotts and Orchard Road, Isetan Wisma on Orchard Road, Isetan Katong in Parkway Parade and Isetan Tampines in Tampines Mall. Isetan has a cosmetics and fragrance section, shoes, sportswear, women's and men's fashion as well accessories. Although Isetan Scotts and Isetan Wisma are across the street from each other, they cater to slightly different markets; Isetan Scotts' focus is on younger adults while Isetan Wisma carries fashion labels Emporio Armani, Paul Smith and local brand Song + Kelly 21. 🚇 Orchard, Map p.282 B3 **24**

John Little

6737 2222

Various locations

www.johnlittle.com.sg

Established in 1845 and acquired by Robinsons in 1955, this department store chain has seven stores in Singapore at Specialists' Shopping Centre on Orchard Road, Plaza Singapura (p.176), Compass Point, North Point, White Sands, Causeway Point and Jurong Point. It is famed for its housewares and wide range of women's and men's fashion.

Robinson's

6733 0888

Centrepoint Centre, Orchard   www.centrepoint.com.sg

Founded in 1858, Robinson and Spicer originally sold basic foodstuff. You'll find the flagship store at Centrepoint (p.172) on Orchard Road, with another store at Raffles City (p.177). Perhaps what truly sets this department store apart is the level of service and its employees' loyalty. Floor staff are known to stay on the job for up to 20 years and service is impeccable. The sales here are also legendary. ⬛ Somerset, Map p.283 E4 **6**

Takashimaya

6738 1111

Ngee Ann City, Orchard   www.takashimaya-sin.com

Open from 10:00 to 21:30 every day bar Chinese New Year, Takashimaya has seven floors chock-a-block with fashion, housewares, cosmetics, toys, luggage, jewellery, restaurants and even a gym complete with pool and Jacuzzi. You can sample almost every type of Asian cuisine in the food court housed in the basement. ⬛ Somerset, Map p.282 C4 **25**

Tangs

6737 5500

310 Orchard Rd, Orchard,   www.tangs.com

Tangs was started when a Chinese immigrant arrived in Singapore in 1932, armed with a chest of goods to sell. He then parlayed his business into a department store. In 2004 Tangs was given a facelift and emerged as a high-end, award-winning department store with boutique fashion, fragrance and cosmetics. For a break there's the Island Java Bar on the third floor and an Island Cafe on the fourth. The basement also houses an enticing food hall. ⬛ Orchard, Map p.282 B3 **26**

Books

If you're an avid or eclectic reader, you've landed in the right place. In the heart of Orchard Road, in Wheelock Place, Borders (6235 7146) is a literary fan's idea of heaven (and even if you're not, you might find a sudden attack of enthusiasm coming on when you hear that a local women's magazine voted it one of the best places to pick up a girl or guy). Borders also stocks stationery, mostly from UK's Paperchase, magazines and a selection of music CDs and DVDs. Attached to it is a cafe that serves decent lattes, cakes, pastas and pizzas. The cafe also has liquor licence and an alfresco area.

Kinokuniya is one of the largest chains of bookshops in south-east Asia, and of its three outlets in Singapore, the one in Ngee Ann City (p.174) is huge. It has over 500,000 book titles in various languages, and being a Japanese chain, it has a large Japanese section including shelves of manga. It also houses a Coffee Bean & Tea Leaf and serves up a wide selection of international and local magazines. You'll also find Page One (6272 0822) at VivoCity (p.179), a speciality bookshop that carries high quality coffee table books and even music scores.

Times The Bookshop and MPH are the two oldest homegrown chains of bookshops in Singapore. MPH was established in 1895 and Times in 1968. They stock mostly bestsellers, management and self-help books and popular magazines. Other chains that remain firm favourites with Singaporeans are Harris, who have two stores, and Popular, who have outlets all over the city-state as well as a great online shop.

Camera Equipment

Singapore is one of the best places in the world to buy cameras and peripheries. Taxes on electronics are low and if you're just visiting, you can get a rebate off the GST.

Keen shutterbugs should head straight to The Peninsula Plaza, Peninsula Shopping Centre and the Adelphi (map p.290 B3). They're across the road from one another and most shops in this area are trustworthy. They'll give you a fair price partly because of the keen competition, and partly because they're run by enthusiasts.

Cathay Photo Store (6337 4274) at Peninsula Plaza is one outlet in a chain that sells all major brands of cameras and accessories. Over 40 years old, it's a well-known hangout for professional and amateur photographers. Alan Photo Trading (6336 0922) at Sim Lim Square is also well established and offers the widest range of photographic supplies including popular brands and models of SLRs and digital cameras. John 3:16 (6337 2877) at Funan Centre is another good shop for professional photography equipment and accessories.

If a digital pocket camera is what you want, simply head to the nearest electronic chain store. Harvey Norman, Best Denki and Courts have locations across Singapore consistently quote fair prices and you won't have to haggle for hours to get a good deal. You could also price the object of your desire at an electronics chain store and then call or visit Alan Photo Trading or Paris Silk (6466 6002) in Holland Village (p.169) to compare quotes. If you're up for a good bargaining session, head down to Sim Lim Square, the electronics Mecca of Singapore. If you do walk away with a prize from here though, be sure to get receipts and the right warranty cards. Some stores offer Singapore-only warranties or no warranty at all.

Be aware that some camera models can differ too – certain models of digital camera from Sony, for example, are only released in Europe and Asia, so if you're buying a camera to use in North America, it might be a challenge to get it fixed there. For camera repairs, the most reputable shop in town is probably the Camera Workshop (6336 1956) at Peninsula Shopping Centre.

Souvenirs

There are no quintessential souvenirs from Singapore per se, unless you're looking for the standard 'Merlion' key chains and Singapore Airlines lookalike uniforms, in which case head straight to Chinatown, Arab Street (p.168) or Little India (p.169). Here you'll find Merlion caps, pens, tiger balm and of course, T-shirts including those with the infamous 'Singapore is a fine city' across the front. If you're looking for something more subtle, stop in at the Risis Boutique (6338 8250) at Suntec City (p.178). Risis use a process that enables them to dip fresh orchids into 24 carat gold and turn them into brooches, necklaces and tie clips.

Museum shops in the various museums in town are also good places to hunt for Singapore-inspired souvenirs like old Peranakan tiles that have been made into coasters and pretty watercolour paintings of the Singapore skyline. DFS Galleria (6735 4525) in Orchard also has the ubiquitous tiger balm and chopsticks nicely packaged as souvenirs.

Tailoring

Walk into Far East Plaza, Far East Shopping Centre or Lucky Plaza along Orchard Road and, if you look like a tourist, you'll be accosted by shop owners asking if you want a suit made in 24 hours. Most will make you a suit for under $200 or a shirt for $80 (after a little bargaining) and they're good if you are not too choosy or don't have much time.

If you're looking for better quality (and don't mind paying more) be prepared to wait as tailors are in high demand. Do keep in mind that fabrics here are all imported so tailoring is not quite the bargain it is in Bangkok or Hong Kong.

Anson Tailors (6224 1572) near Chinatown have been making suits for smartly turned out clients (like CEOs who need to cut a dash or TV stars) since 1955 and they use excellent fabrics including Zegna wool. A suit will cost from $2,000 to $5,000 here.

CYC (6336 3556) is a custom shirt shop that's been making shirts for former Prime Minister Lee Kuan Yew for decades. Customers can choose from more than a thousand fabrics, 60 collars and 10 styles of cuffs. Shirts cost about $75 and take around 10 days to make.

Most women go to one of the speciality wedding shops to have their fancy evening dresses made. The *Tatler* set, when not wearing Versace and Gucci, go to local designers Heng Nam Nam (6227 8023) or Frederick Li (6323 4372) who also make wedding dresses. Mode-O-Day (6235 1418) is also popular with young socialites and apparently Bill and Hillary Clinton had clothes tailored by them when they stepped into town.

Going Out

Introduction

Singaporeans are obsessed with eating. From hawker centres to haute cuisine, you'll find the city packed with fantastic variety to suit every budget.

If you like eating out, with a special penchant for Asian cuisine, you have come to the right place. Singaporeans often replace 'how are you?' with 'have you eaten?'. To eat well is, by their standards, to be well. And as with Malaysians, there is nothing unusual here about discussing the next meal while you eat the current one. Food here is not only good but it is available at all hours in hygienic surroundings, so experimentation is highly encouraged. And while there are named gourmet restaurants, the right local morsel can be almost as fantastic, for as little as two dollars.

People in Singapore eat out a lot, and the dining scene is always developing and changing. From the street corner hawker stalls to the finest French restaurants, there is a lot of variety. Understandably, the city-state is best for those who enjoy Asian food. The variety of localised cuisines; Chinese, Malay, Indian, Thai, Vietnamese is superb – to the extent that local people will refer you to the exact dish or must-try and where to have it. And low and behold, when you arrive, there is a queue for that exact dish.

The fact that Singaporeans are often as hip, if not more, than expats and visitors to the city makes the nightlife fun. As does the fact that seeing an ang moh (Chinese for foreigner) is no big deal. This relative equality and anonymity is refreshing for south-east Asia, as is a culture becoming more permissive and accepting of modern vices such as alcohol, sex and (more recently) gambling, plus partying until the wee hours.

Drinking

You may find it expensive, as alcohol is heavily taxed, so don't be surprised to pay $14 for a pint of beer. But competition in the bar scene is alive and well, so do look out for specials including generous happy hours and 'two-for-one' nights. Drinking a lot and getting rowdy is fine here too, although really 'losing it', so to speak, particularly if you get confrontational, is as frowned upon here as it is in most Asian countries. The upside of this is that Singapore is a relatively safe place to go out, and for women in particular, the ability to move around the well-populated areas at night without feeling at risk is a real plus to living here.

Alcohol is widely available throughout Singapore, outside places of worship and halal establishments. You can buy beer, wine and spirits in supermarkets and 7-Eleven stores until late, and outlets selling drinks range from coffee shops or hawker stalls to world-class bars with a wide selection of international brands.

You must be over 18 to drink, and outlets may request photo ID on admission. Also remember that Singapore operates a zero-tolerance policy on drink driving with hefty punishments for those found intoxicated. The police put up regular roadblocks late at night to catch offenders, so consider yourself warned. If you've had a tipple (or seven) take a taxi. They are good value, safe and abundant.

Vegetarian Food

The best place to start for vegetarians is local cuisine. Among Singapore's mix of cuisine styles many Indians are vegetarians, while Thai and Vietnamese cuisines in particular have a lot of non-meat choices.

On the other hand, Chinese restaurants may tell you that a dish is vegetarian, only for you to find a bit of pork floating in it, so always double check before you order. However, there are some Chinese restaurants that are completely vegetarian, serving a range of mock-meat dishes from duck and fish to a whole suckling pig, fairly close in taste and resemblance to the real thing, but made entirely of gluten.

Specialist western vegetarian restaurants are less common but for award-winning Mediterranean food that even non-vegetarians rave about, try Original Sin in Holland Village (p.258). For those who like to include fish as part as their diet, Singapore has a wide variety of fish and seafood outlets throughout the city. In food

The Yellow Star

This natty yellow star is our way of highlighting places that we think merit extra praise. It could be the atmosphere, the food, the cocktails, the music or the crowd – but whatever the reason, any review that you see with the star attached is somewhere that we think is a bit special.

Ministry of Sound

courts, try the Yong Tao Foo stalls, where you can load up your own plates with fish balls and vegetables.

Peranakan Food

Peranakans, or nonyas, were Chinese immigrants that settled along the Straits of Malaya and inter-married with indigenous Malays. Nonya food has a peculiarly difficult taste to establish and, unless spot-on, becomes either Chinese or Malay food or simply unrecognisable. Nonyas are renowned for being insufferably fastidious about how their food tastes and many seldom eat their cuisine in a restaurant, preferring to cook it themselves. For chances to sample this cuisine, try Guan Hoe Soon Restaurant (p.221) or Blue Ginger (p.199).

Venue Directory

CBD, Marina Bay & Suntec

Waterside entertainment and some very fine dining perfectly complement the stunning views downtown.

This buzzing financial district has become, in recent years, the place to live, work and play. The redevelopment of the riverside has resulted in some exceptional restaurants, many of which are in the luxury hotels that overlook the water – the ideal place to watch the sun set with a cocktail in hand.

Venue Finder

Restaurants

Al Dente Trattoria

Italian

Esplanade, Marina Bay

6341 9188

Al Dente Trattoria is the perfect place to grab a bite before or after a performance at the Esplanade Theatres on the Bay. The best seats in the house are on the roof-top patio, where enchanting views unfold in front of you. The menu is predominantly Italian and the staff are more than happy to recommend dishes, and help match them with a wine from the extensive list. 🚇 City Hall, Map p.291 D4 **1**

Blue Ginger

Singaporean

97 Tanjong Pagar Rd, Tanjong Pagar

6222 3928

The restaurant gives a sense of being in a wealthy Peranakan home and the cuisine is no more than common home-cooked fare typical to Peranakans. What distinguishes Blue Ginger is the quality of the food, made possible by the freshest, finest ingredients available. It's best to go in a group so you can order more dishes. The perennial favourite is ayam buah keluak, braised chicken flavoured with turmeric, galangal and lemongrass, cooked with Indonesian black nuts. 🚇 Tanjong Pagar, Map p.295 F4 **2**

Creperie Ar-Men

French

37 Duxton Rd, Tanjong Pagar

6227 3389

This authentic French creperie from Brittany gets appreciative nods from the French community living here. Both food and ambience transport you to a cosy diner on the coast of Brittany where cuisine is marked by simplicity, a lack of pomp, and high-quality ingredients. The sweet and savoury crepes are as simple as butter, honey and lemon and others as elaborate as the croix alpine comprising potatoes, onion and bacon cooked in white wine sauce, with reblochon cheese sauce. A visit is made all the more worthwhile by the modest prices. 🚇 Tanjong Pagar, Map p.295 F4 **3**

Hai Tien Lo
Chinese
Pan Pacific Hotel, Marina Bay
6826 8338

Encapsulated by full-length glass windows 37 floors above the Marina Bay, Hai Tien Lo has maintained its reputation as one of Singapore's premier sky dining restaurants. The decor, with a crisp, modern Chinese ambience, perfectly complements the culinary creativity of its chef, the dynamic Lai Tong Ping who immaculately presents signature dishes such as fried imperial swiftlet's nest in egg white and fillet of cod in Japanese sake sauce. 🚇 City Hall, Map p.291 E3 **4**

Keyaki
Japanese
Pan Pacific Hotel, Marina Bay
6826 8335

Set in the centre of an immaculate garden, this fine dining Japanese restaurant is authentically modelled after a Meiji-era Japanese farmhouse. Keyaki offers the full spectrum of Japanese food, from the popular sushi, tempura and teriyaki to Japanese haute cuisine. Weekend lunches, where for a fixed price you may order as much as you want from the a la carte menu, are often family affairs where young children are welcome. 🚇 City Hall, Map p.291 E3 **4**

Lau Pa Sat Food Centre

Hawker Centres

18 Raffles Quay, CBD

Built in 1894,Lau Pa Sat is the largest remaining Victorian filigree cast-iron structure in south-east Asia. On the south side, the satay stalls on the street are popular and delicious, and many customers choose the tables on the street for this reason. One stall in particular, Fatman Satay, is a local favourite. Inside, the Indian food is among the best – you could do a lot worse than a masala dosai set here. ⬛ Raffles Place, Map p.296 B3 **5**

Oscar's

International

Conrad Centennial, Suntec

6432 7481

The appeal of the Californian-styled Oscar's is its classy simplicity, with a rich array of cuisine options amid a breezy and busy, yet friendly, ambience. With three packed buffets a day, this comfortable 24 hour diner is great for those on the run. Try the sumptuous laksa with fat king prawns or excellent noodle dishes such as mee goreng and char kway teow, each served with tasty sambal. ⬛ City Hall, Map p.291 E3 **6**

Paulaner Bräuhaus Singapore

German

9 Raffles Blvd, Marina Bay

6883 2572

Paulander Bräuhaus's focal point is its very ornate, and very German, in-house microbrewery. If you have a group of 10 to 15, ask and the resident brew master will take you on a tour with tastings. When it comes to the grub, the menu is split into Continental and German specialities such as pork knuckles and Nurnberger Bratwurst with sauerkraut, which are not to be missed. ⬛ City Hall, Map p.291 E3 **7**

Pierside Kitchen
International
6438 0400

1 Fullerton Rd, Marina Bay

This stylish waterfront restaurant and bar offers stunning views of the river and bay, and the subdued lighting and music complement the distinctive pared-down decor of modern clean lines – leaving one to focus on the food. The menu, focusing on seafood, is truly international, with an emphasis on the freshest possible ingredients. The entire dining experience is consistently high and the wine list is impeccable. 🚇 City Hall, Map p.296 C1 **8**

Rang Mahal
Indian
6333 1788

Pan Pacific Hotel, Marina Bay

Once ranked as one of the world's top 100 restaurants by *Condé Nast* magazine, Rang Mahal takes Indian cuisine to a level you've probably never seen before. The presentation is very modern, matching the hip interior and smooth down-tempo Indian beats in the background. There's a choice of a la carte, tasting and gastronome menus, as well as wine or whiskey matched menus and a lunchtime buffet. Reservations recommended. 🚇 City Hall, Map p.291 E3 **4**

SH Tours
Dinner Cruises
6734 9923

100 Kim Seng Rd, River Valley Road

SH Tours offers the popular Starlite Dinner Cruise, where you can spend the evening cruising the waters of Singapore aboard a traditional Chinese junk, with a Singaporean buffet dinner and live music for extra entertainment. This cruise departs daily from Clifford Pier at 18:00 and costs $39 for

Riverside dining

adults and $20 for children under 12. Embarkation is 15 minutes before departure. 🚇 Outram Park, Map p.296 C2 **9**

Silk Road

Chinese

Amara Hotel, Telok Blangah

6227 3848

Travellers have journeyed the Silk Road spanning China for trade, adventure or a walk through history. If you wish to travel it for the food, then you need go no further than the Silk Road restaurant. Warm, neutral colours and dim, soothing lights create a contemporary and dignified mood. Pair your food with an aromatic eight-treasure tea, prepared by a tea master using a copper kettle with a metre long spout, or with a Chinese wine. 🚇 Tanjong Pagar, Map p.279 D3 **10**

ThaiExpress

Thai

Colours By The Bay, Marina Bay

6533 6766

Tasty and well-priced, ThaiExpress is a good, mid-priced chain with 15 outlets in Singapore. The secret is excellent recipes and good choices, including a number of relatively nutritious dishes like mango salads and grilled meat. Excellent for its laksa, curries and street-food inspired favourites, ThaiExpress is in fact relatively regional in its influences. Buy a few dishes and share, Asian-style. 🚇 City Hall, Map p.291 D4 **11**

Via Mar

Spanish

Esplanade, Marina Bay

6423 0900

Via Mar provides an extensive tapas selection and a good a la carte menu of main courses. The indoor dining area is lit for a romantic mood but most patrons opt for the spacious alfresco area. The lunch specials are excellent value, but highlight of the week has to be Tuesday's Senora's Night when ladies pay $35 and men $52 for an eat-as-much-as-you-can tapas menu plus free-flowing house wines and Carlsberg on draft. 🖼 City Hall, Map p.291 D4 **1**

Bars & Pubs

Balaclava
Suntec City Convention Ctr, Suntec

Bar

65339 1600

Long in need of a decent early evening bar, Suntec City now boasts one of Singapore's best. Balaclava is large and laid back, packed with office workers on Friday evening in particular. The cool interior features lots of red, lamps and divides, mixing timber, leather and silk. With a good indoor and outdoor mix of seating, it's a good bet after a busy day out, or before the next bar. 🖼 City Hall, Map p.291 E3 **12**

Nightclubs

Coco Latte
Gallery Hotel, CBD

Nightclub

6736 3208

An alternative rock bar, Coco Latte's ground floor has some of the best, edgy interior-decorating of any club in Singapore and its ground floor is a fusion of funky artwork. Follow the winding staircase up this unique circular-shaped bar and you'll reach the second floor, which is dedicated to dancing. With hip-hop, indie and other genres pumping out, the small dance floor gets packed on busy nights. 🖼 Clarke Quay, Map p.289 D4 **13**

Chinatown

With fantastic food and atmosphere, Chinatown's streets make for great culinary exploring at night.

While searching among the stalls and hawker centres for your new favourite dish is the common Chinatown experience, you'll be pleased to find a variety of cuisines available in this area, as well as the popular Crazy Elephant pub (p.210).

For authentic eating head straight to Maxwell Food Centre which is a local favourite and therefore particularly popular at lunchtimes, so be warned. If your tastebuds are after something a little more sophisticated, then the Italian menu at San Marco (p.209) at The Fullerton won't disappoint, but you'll have to reserve a table.

After dark, the former fishing village of Tanjong Pagar turns from a bustling shopping area to a vibrant party place filled with thriving cafes, pubs, gay bars and restaurants and it's prime people-watching territiory.

Venue Finder

The Moomba	Australian	p.208
Oosters Belgian Brasserie	European	p.209
Maxwell Food Centre ✦	Hawker Centre	p.208
Mozzaic ✦	International	p.209
Da Paolo e Judie ✦	Italian	p.207
San Marco	Italian	p.209
Senso	Italian	p.210
Crazy Elephant ✦	Pub	p.210

San Marco

Restaurants

Da Paolo e Judie
Italian

81 Neil Rd, Chinatown
6225 8306

Bring a healthy appetite to this fine dining establishment; you'll need it for the generous portions. Mouthwatering northern Italian cuisine including seafood and freshly-made pasta is on offer but leave room for dessert, the chocolate lava cake is to die for. You may bring your own wine (corkage fee of $35) but why bother when you can choose from a wide-ranging array of wines personally selected by Paolo Scarpa himself? 🚇 Chinatown, Map p.295 E4 **14**

Ikukan
Japanese

23 Mohd Ali Lane, Chinatown
6325 3362

This quaint little restaurant off Club Street is a delight to visit; serving up contemporary Japanese cuisine alongside the chef's unique creations. The menu offers items such as black winter truffles with mizuna and prosciutto, creme brulee with oolong poached pears, and a great yakitori selection. There are some very reasonably-priced lunch sets or you could opt for one of the special set meals, which gives you a chance to sample more of the menu. ⬛ Tanjong Pagar, Map p.296 A2 **15**

Maxwell Food Centre
Hawker Centre

Maxwell Rd, Chinatown

Chosen by residents as the best hawker centre in a recent survey, Maxwell is heralded by many in the know as having the 'best chicken rice' in the country. Open 24 hours and always busy, it is not the most comfortable, but the taste, variety and of exotic nature of its dishes makes up for it. Take your pick, but the local nasi padang (rice and your selection of dishes on top) is essential eating. ⬛ Chinatown, Map p.295 F3 **16**

The Moomba
Australian

52 Circular Rd, Chinatown
6438 0141

Huge, vibrant Aboriginal paintings and motifs decorate this warm and cosy restaurant converted from a two-storey shophouse. Characteristic of modern Australian cuisine, the food is unfussy, light and refreshing with a focus on clever combinations of herbs and vegetables. Try the barbecued kangaroo loin with a white truffle infused soya glaze and wasabi potato mash. All menu items come with a wine recommendations, mainly an Australian or New Zealand option. 🚇 Chinatown, Map p.296 B1 **17**

Mozzaic   International
36 Club St, Chinatown   6325 3360

This relaxed eatery's USP is its unusual, eclectic mix of three very different and unrelated cuisines – Japanese, European and Brazilian. The churrasco is good value for money at $38 for unlimited servings sliced straight from the skewers and the tasty roast simmered duck, served cold with a mushroom and leek salad, is also recommended. The cheery interior with clean lines provides for a slightly up-market atmosphere, ideal for degustation. 🚇 Chinatown, Map p.296 A2 **18**

Oosters Belgian Brasserie   European
25 Church St, Chinatown   6438 3210

Popular with the Raffles Place crowd, Oosters has a whole section on the menu dedicated to the mussel, and they are truly not to be missed. You can order them in 500g or 1kg increments in a variety of ways, topped with gruyere cheese or served in tom yam soup. To complete the experience, Oosters has Leffe beer on tap, in addition to a range of Abbey and Trappist and artisan beers. 🚇 Raffles Place, Map p.296 B2 **19**

San Marco   Italian
The Fullerton, Chinatown   6438 4404

Situated in the old lighthouse in the majestic Fullerton Hotel, San Marco is an intimate, minimalist restaurant with stunning views of the sea. The quality of service is rare – plates are cleared before you even realise they're empty – and the pacing of the dishes is faultless. The 10 course degustation menu is well worth trying and despite the number of dishes, you will not be left too full to detract from the pleasure of the experience. 🗺 Raffles Place, Map p.296 C1 **20**

Senso
21 Club St, Chinatown

Italian
6224 3534

You get the complete Italian experience at this former convent from the architecture and decor to the food and wine. There are three main areas, each with a different ambience; the bar is uber-hip and modern, the main dining area is both cosy and corporate and the courtyard dining area transports you to southern Italy. In spite of the restaurant being so swanky, it is still a place where you can immediately relax. 🗺 Chinatown, Map p.296 A2 **21**

Bars & Pubs

Crazy Elephant
3E River Valley Rd, Chinatown

Pub
6337 1990

One of Singapore's best established live music venues, Crazy Elephant is the home of loud pub blues, graffitied walls, and a maverick attitude all its own – witnessed by the crude jokes that circulate on the television. Undergoing a renaissance thanks to the resurrection of Clarke Quay, Crazy Elephant is one of those pubs that hasn't changed – and can rightly claim it doesn't need to. 🗺 Clarke Quay, Map p.290 A4 **22**

Clockwise from top left: Chinatown, Dining outdoors local style, Senso

Colonial District

The historical heart of Singapore has many modern offerings but you might want to step back in time, too.

With Raffles Hotel setting the tone, the Colonial District is a must visit for its heritage alone. Add some culture, outstanding restaurants and knock-out views into the mix and this is an area of Singapore that you simply must experience. High tea in the Tiffin Room (p.216) is a longstanding tradition but for new, dizzying heights head straight up to Jaan (p.214) where you'll see the island laid out before you.

Venue Finder

Long Bar Steakhouse

Restaurants

Empire Café
Raffles Hotel, Colonial District

Singaporean
6412 1101

Not to be dismissed as just another hotel offering a bourgeois take on hawker favourites, the Empire Café makes for a good pit stop if you are in the area. Enjoy hainanese chicken rice, roti prata, spring rolls, beef noodles and chili prawns within the air-conditioned interior of the cafe – built to resemble the kopitiams, or coffee shops, from a few decades back. Although the prices are not lost on the location, the standard of the food here is worth it. Also check out Ah Teng's Bakery next door, which offers some very good icecream, cakes, cookies and pastries. ⬛ City Hall, Map p.291 D2 ㉓

Inagiku
Japanese

Raffles The Plaza, Colonial District 6431 6156

One of the more spacious high-end Japanese restaurants, Inagiku has a sushi bar, a teppanyaki counter and a tempura bar set in three different parts of the restaurant, as well as a separate main dining area. The decor is surprisingly ordinary for such an expensive restaurant, but the extraordinary quality of the sashimi and sushi makes up for it. The menu is extensive and the dishes are prepared in a traditional manner. 🚇 City Hall, Map p.290 C2 24

Jaan
French

Swissôtel The Stamford, Colonial District 6837 3322

There are few restaurants in Singapore offering as spectacular a view of the city as Jaan. Perched atop the highest hotel on the island, the view from the 70th floor is inspiring. The cuisine is modern French and the menu changes seasonally or according to the irrepressibly creative flair of Chef Michael Muller. When it comes to wine, you'll be wise to ask for recommendations: the homework has been done and the matching is splendid. 🚇 City Hall, Map p.290 C3 25

Lei Gardens
Chinese

30 Victoria St, Colonial District 6339 3822

With a list of awards that reads as long as some menus, Lei Gardens is regarded as an institution among Chinese restaurants. The dishes are light, refined and express the best of traditional Cantonese cooking. Catering to the well-heeled, the restaurant isn't sparing in the use of expensive ingredients (including seahorse), nor the time taken to prepare dishes; and the result justifies the means. City Hall, Map p.290 C2 **26**

Long Bar Steakhouse
Steakhouses
Raffles Hotel, Colonial District
6412 1307

While in Singapore you can't miss the world-famous Raffles Hotel, and a meal at the Long Bar Steakhouse makes your visit even more special. The menu features premium steaks and seafood grilled to perfection, with an Asian touch of local spices. There are set dinners for two including surf & turf and the steakhouse grill. For dessert, don't miss the sago coconut jelly with papaya, macadamia, pandan cream, and gula melaka icecream, a true Raffles original. City Hall, Map p.291 D2 **23**

Pizzeria Giardino
Italian
Chijmes, Colonial District
6338 8711

If you can picture yourself eating truffle-laced ravioli amidst lush lawns and fairy-lit trees, then this is the place for you. Relaxed and friendly, the energetic staff and smooth tunes conspire to create a convivial atmosphere that attracts couples and groups alike. Best known for its delicious wood-fried pizzas, the kitchen also produces a range of tasty Italian dishes at reasonable prices alongside classic favourites. It does pay to arrive early, as this venue does fill up. City Hall, Map p.290 C2 **26**

Raffles Grill
French
Raffles Hotel, Colonial District
6337 1886

Restored to its resplendent glory, at the heart of this grand hotel is the Raffles Grill – the mother of French haute cuisine in Singapore. This formal restaurant, where a dinner jacket is highly appropriate, exudes the elegant luxury that lent the old world its charm, and where traditional, classic French-style cooking is truly at home. The service is immaculate and the wine list offers classic vintages from as far back as 1900. City Hall, Map p.291 D2 23

Table 108
Singaporean
Chijmes, Colonial District
6338 6108

It is the location rather than the menu that makes Table 108 the perfect choice for visitors to Singapore. With a lively outdoor setting heightened by the buzz of surrounding restaurants and bars, this is a venue best frequented in the evening, where you will find yourself dining at the foot of the floodlit Chijmes cathedral. Table 108 also offers a sumptuous red lanterned indoor setting and small but chic martini bar where you can enjoy a drink before or after your grilled stingray or prawn mee soup. City Hall, Map p.290 C2 27

Tiffin Room
International
Raffles Hotel, New Asia
6412 1194

The Tiffin Room is an integral dining experience for many tourists and visitors to Raffles Hotel and Singapore. Billed as 'one of the oldest traditions' in Singapore's historic hotel, Tiffin Room is a study of delicate and quietly ornate tropical colonial decor, beautifully preserved from the early 1890's, contrasting with a bright, open and relaxed atmosphere. Open from breakfast through to high tea and dinner, all dining requirements are catered for. City Hall, Map p.291 D2 23

Vansh

Indian

Marina Square, Colonial District   6345 4466

While 'modern Indian' is often interpreted as 'fusion food', Vansh remains true to traditional Indian cuisine. Making its mark with stylish presentation and some distinctive dishes, the menu remains true to traditional Indian cuisine. Set on the water by the Kallang River, this is a great place to relax with friends. The vibe is very funky, with loungy, comfortable furniture and a separate bar area at the back that is ideal for drinks. It is pleasantly quiet during the week, but picks up on weekends, so reservations are recommended. 🚇 City Hall, Map p.291 E4 **29**

Viet Lang

Vietnamese

1 Old Parliament Lane, Colonial District   6337 3379

Located in the oldest government building on the island, the Empress Place, Viet Lang's alfresco dining space allows you to soak in both the old and new worlds of this cosmopolitan city. The menu has a repertoire spanning north, central and south Vietnam, so you will get popular favourites as well as elaborate dishes, all made with ingredients and condiments imported direct from Vietnam. 🚇 Raffles Place, Map p.290 B4 **30**

Cafes

Menotti

Cafe

Raffles City Shopping Centre, Colonial District   6333 9366

Picture Italian high fashion applied to a cafe and you've got Menotti, a truly authentic Italian eatery. The decor is slick, modern and chic. Seating is both indoor and outdoor, from 10:00 to midnight. The menu is traditional from the coffees, pastries, cakes, snacks to breakfast, lunch and dinner meals. No suprises other than the exceptional quality and authenticity. The two course set lunch is excellent value, with choices as tagliatelle with king scallops or linguine with blue swimmer crab. 🚇 City Hall, Map p.290 C3 **31**

Bars & Pubs

New Asia Bar & Grill
Bar

Swissôtel The Stamford, Colonial District   6431 5672

From its vantage point 226 metres up in The Stamford, this bar offers views over Singapore and the nearby Indonesian islands. With the gleaming skyline in front of you and a chocolate cocktail in your hand you really will be living the high life. With house music, bright colours and even a slanting floor (for optimum views of course), this is a bar experience you'll never forget. 🚇 City Hall, Map p.290 C3 **25**

Timbre Music Bistro
Bar

Armenian St, Colonial District   6338 8277

Out the back of the Substation Theatre, Timbre Music Bistro opened in late 2005 to re-establish the tree-lined courtyard as the city's coolest spot for live indie music. Dotted with wooden outdoor tables under the trees, there is a warm, contemporary feel, and it often plays host to acoustic bands. Alongside the music, they serve up a tasty selection of bistro meals, cocktails and cold beer, with the upscale nature of the space reflecting the maturity of the artsy crowd. 🚇 City Hall, Map p.290 B2 **33**

East Coast

Seafood waits at every turn on the coast and Singaporeans wouldn't have it any other way.

Sea views, palm trees and fresh crab all conspire to make the East Coast a laidback destination for food fans. Aside from the ever-popular seafood, you'll also find traditional Peranakan food at Guan Hoe Soon Restaurant (p.221) where residents have been coming for generations, and the reasonable prices and extensive menu make it a great starting point for exploring this famed cuisine.

Other options include the inexpensive hawker centre in Changi Village which serves a fantastic nasi lemak (a Malay dish of fish, chicken and peanuts) while its carpark offers the curious a chance to ogle the friendly transsexual men.

Venue Finder

Blue Lobster	Seafood	p.221
Guan Hoe Soon	Singaporean	p.221
Jumbo Seafood	Seafood	p.221
Lemongrass	Thai	p.222
Mushroom Pot	Chinese	p.222

Restaurants

Blue Lobster   Seafood
87 Frankel Ave, Siglap   6442 5090

Blue Lobster is a little gem where seafood dishes take
centre stage in the small but intense menu. The restaurant
has a cosy feel to it, with a front patio for relaxed alfresco
dining and intimate booths inside. Chef Karl Dobler creates
extraordinary dishes with a variety of fish and shellfish that
highlight his European, Asian and Australian influences.
Finish by exploring the extensive and decadent dessert
menu. 🚇 Kembangan, Map p.277 E3

Guan Hoe Soon Restaurant   Singaporean
214 Joo Chiat Rd, East Coast   6344 2761

Still run by the original Yap family who own the restaurant,
Guan Hoe Soon has offered high quality Peranakan cuisine
since 1953. The original recipes have been tweaked slightly
for today's health conscious customers, with less salt and
oil, but the food is still authentic, the prices moderate and
the decor functionally plain. Try the ayam buah keluak,
babi pong tay, itek tim, chap chye, hee peow soup and beef
rendang. 🚇 Paya Lebar, Map p.279 F2 35

Jumbo Seafood   Seafood
East Coast Seafood Centre, East Coast   6442 3435

A great place to enjoy some of Singapore's most famous
dishes, Jumbo Seafood has five branches around the city,
including one in the East Coast Seafood Centre. Signature

dishes include red Sri Lankan crab in rich chilli gravy or white pepper crab in a black peppery gravy. An evening at Jumbo is a messy experience – expect to get your hands enjoyably dirty, and to get some exercise as you crack into the thick crab shells. 🚇 Bedok, Map p.277 E3

Lemongrass

Thai

899 East Coast Rd, East Coast

6443 1995

Lemongrass is a mid-priced Thai restaurant with more than 60 dishes on its main menu and another 20 on a separate vegetarian menu. The food is tasty, down-to-earth and typical of what middle-class Thais eat everyday. The interior is purposely designed to be simple, old-fashioned and reminiscent of a period that has been all but erased by modernity. There is an alfresco option, but with only a few tables, reservations are necessary. 🚇 Kembangan, Map p.277 E3

Mushroom Pot

Chinese

Singapore Indoor Stadium, Kallang

6342 3320

The first of its kind in Singapore, the Mushroom Pot offers novel Chinese fusion dishes featuring more than 20 types of delicious and rare, imported and wild mushrooms – which contain healing properties and are high in protein, minerals and vitamins. Signature dishes include sliced mushrooms and potatoes covered with fish roe and melted cheese or codfish topped with matsutake mushrooms and a tangy sauce with a touch of curry. One must-try is the mushroom hot pot (steamboat) which allows you to savour a variety of mushrooms in one dish. 🚇 Kallang, Map p.279 E2 38

豬什湯 卤豬腳

巴生肉骨茶

鴨啟#3 里面／甲鳥麥面 $2.50

Little India & Arab Street

Rich colours, enticing smells and vibrant crowds make these ethnic areas irresistible.

Spicing up your stay is easy with Singapore's diverse communities. While chaotic at times, Little India keeps on attracting non-Indians; heady promises of vegetarian fare, plump prawns served on a banana leaf and glasses of fresh lassi are too much to resist.

It it's a Middle Eastern food fix you're after then the stalls along Arab Street (map p.285 E4) won't disappoint and the shisha cafes complete the experience. With a trip to this part of town it's almost like another holiday.

Venue Finder

Komala Vilas	Indian	p.225
Raj Restaurant	Indian	p.225
Garibaldi	Italian	p.225
Pitch Black	Cafe	p.226

Restaurants

Garibaldi
Italian

36 Purvis Street, Colonial District   6837 1468

Despite a formal first impression, Garibaldi is one of Singapore's most popular Italian fine dining restaurants. The food is the primary attraction, and dishes are carefully crafted using authentic Italian ingredients, many flown in from Italy, with the flavours and textures beautifully balanced. Dishes worth trying include the lamb tenderloin with porcini mushrooms and balsamico sauce; or, if in season, the white truffle pasta. It also has one of the finest wine lists in Singapore. 🚇 City Hall, Map p.291 D2 **39**

Komala Vilas

Indian

76-78 Serangoon Rd, Little India   6293 6980

One of the archetypal experiences of Little India, Komala Vilas has been serving authentic Indian vegetarian food since 1947. With dishes like onion dosa with sliced onion filling, a snip at $2.40; tomato uttappam (pancake with tomato spread) for $2.50; or a samosa plate-puff with mixed vegetable filling for $1.80, the price and formula work perfectly. Lined with whitewashed walls, sit at simple tables and enjoy people watching at this busy, egalitarian institution. 🚇 Little India, Map p.284 C2 **40**

Raj Restaurant

Indian

76 Syed Alwi Rd, Little India   6297 1716

Raj offers a spectacular spread of more than 200 northern and southern Indian vegetarian dishes, at prices comparable to other places in the vicinity, but distinctly superior in quality and service. The ambience is warm, relaxed and relatively posh. The chefs are from India, which makes the tastes authentic and more refined than commonly available. You can order a simple plain dosa or chappati meal, right up to rich, creamy paneers and kormas. Great value. 🚇 Little India, Map p.285 E2 **41**

Cafes

Pitch Black

Cafe

63 Haji Lane, Kampong Glam

6392 3457

Pitch Black is part of Singapore's rapidly growing art and cafe scene. The ground floor cafe is inspired industrial chic; harsh concrete and steel with bright colours and black, while upstairs has a mini movie theatre with huge, comfortable sofas. The food is typical cafe fare, such as its homemade sandwiches, with a few creative exceptions; the wild berries chicken and the cheese brownie are well worth trying. A cool place to hang out. 🚇 Bugis, Map p.285 E4 **42**

Hawker Centres & Food Courts

For a true taste of Singapore, you must visit one of these open-air food complexes. The best hawker centres are invariably packed with people queuing for a table and an amazingly-priced variety of food. You'll notice a few standard dishes such as chicken rice, char kway teow (fried flat noodles), wanton mee (dumpling noodles), hokkien fried noodles and chai tau keuh, or fried 'carrot cake'. See Hawker Centres on page 195 for Explorer's top recommendations.

Similar in concept to hawker centres, food courts are indoor, air-conditioned versions. Branches of the two top major chains can often be found in popular malls; Kopitiam (www.kopitiam.biz) and Food Junction (www.foodjunction.com.sg). Picnic Food Court in Scotts Shopping Centre (6734 7560) on Orchard Road is hugely popular because of its central location and excellent choice of food.

Clockwise from top left: Food on display in Little India, Cafe in Arab Street, Little India

Orchard & Tanglin

Orchard Road is the place to see and be seen, whether you're dining alfresco or tucked away in a top hotel.

Amid the shops you'll find some of Singapore's best-loved cafes and restaurants. But if a big night out is on your agenda, then you're in the right spot too, and the luxury hotels put on a great spread for brunches to help you recover the next day.

Venue Finder

Restaurants

BLU
American

Shangri-La Hotel, Orchard   6213 4598

With lovely views high above the Orchard skyline, BLU
has a lovely, hushed jazz club feel, and the menu is one of
Singapore's finest – west coast Americana with a twist of
French flair. Sample the degustation menu for a fine selection
of dishes, or try the Maine lobster paella or the superb cuts of
beef. With a cool, sophisticated atmosphere, BLU has a touch of
the exclusive without feeling stuffy. 🚇 Orchard, Map p.281 F1 **43**

Halia
International

Singapore Botanic Gardens, Tanglin   6476 6711

Located in the beautifully serene Botanic Gardens, Halia is
set amid stunning foliage and colourful flowers. The friendly
service, cosy ambience, and sheer peacefulness makes

it a wonderful place to dine at any time of day or night. The western-asian cuisine has a smart-casual feel at lunch and fine dining at dinner, with dishes such as crisp black pepper soft shell crab or roasted rack of lamb marinated in Javanese spices. For dessert, the cappuccino 'Dunking Pit' is a must try. ▣ Queenstown, Map p.280 B1 **44**

Hard Rock Café   American
50 Cuscaden Rd, Orchard   6235 5232

You won't miss Hard Rock Café, as there's a 1961 Cadillac sitting above the entrance. Expect friendly smiles, awesome service and the full range of American and Tex-Mex mainstays such as sumptuous burgers and sizzling fajitas. The menu is mainly carnivorous, with some seafood thrown into the mix, but there are some vegetarian options and kids will love the atmosphere. At around 22:30 the mood moves up a couple of notches, with a DJ on every night and sometimes a live band. ▣ Orchard, Map p.281 F3 **45**

Harry's Mexican Restaurant & Bar   Mexican
Orchard Parade Hotel, Orchard   6235 5495

Tucked away in the Orchard Parade Hotel, Harry's is a good place to satisfy your craving for Tex-Mex cuisine, and some mean margaritas. The Mexican music can be a bit much on week nights, but it adds to the atmosphere at the weekends when it's busy. The friendly staff are happy to guide you through the menu, and while it caters primarily to hotel guests and office workers on Orchard Road, it's ideal for families too. ▣ Orchard, Map p.281 F2 **46**

Hua Ting
Orchard Hotel, Orchard

Chinese
6734 3880

Winner of numerous prestigious awards, this restaurant is famous for its intricate Asian delicacies and Cantonese specialities. The extensive menu is innovative yet traditional; its most popular dishes cannot be found anywhere else. For dim sum connoisseurs, Hua Ting is paradise. The polished service and informative staff distinguishes Hua Ting from other Chinese restaurants. Reservations maybe required. 🚇 Orchard, Map p.282 A2 47

Iggy's
The Regent, Orchard

European
6733 8888

Acclaimed chef 'Iggy' Chan, who previously worked in three of Singapore's finest kitchens, has set up his own restaurant serving modern European food. There is a small, exclusive dining room and a Japanesestyle counter, where you can choose from three differently priced sets – each changing at the chef's whim and the season. Specialities include wagyu beef hamburger and squid ink risotto, and dishes can be modified to suit individual palates. 🚇 Orchard, Map p.281 E3 48

The Line
Shangri-La Hotel, Orchard

International
6213 4275

The Line is Shangri-La's bold nod to modernist design and gastronomic play, with designer Adam Tihany also responsible for big name restaurants in New York. Shining in white and orange under impressive studio spotlights, the all-you-can-eat buffet features more than 15 cuisines including sushi and sashimi, seafood, noodles, pizzas, dim sum, and items from the wok station or the tandoori oven. Dessert highlights are the icecream teppanyaki, hand rolled in nuts on an iced marble slab, and the metre-high chocolate fountain, waiting for you to dip fat strawberries into. Booking is advised. 🍴 Somerset, Map p.281 F1 **43**

Marmalade Pantry
International

Palais Renaissance, Orchard
6734 2700

This uber-stylish bistro is a favourite with the city's trendy shoppers. Set in an airy, light-filled atrium decorated with steel, mirrors and milk chocolate leather sofas, it has a relaxed and informal atmosphere. The menu is one you'd normally associate more with a fine-dining restaurant; salmon teriyaki with chilled soba, soft shelled crab and rocket, foie gras burgers. Dishes are deliciously innovative, cooked to perfection and all ingredients are exceptionally fresh. The service is friendly and well-polished. 🍴 Orchard, Map p.282 A2 **50**

mezza9
International

Grand Hyatt Singapore, Orchard
6416 7189

The hip and ultra-chic mezzanine floor of the Grand Hyatt offers the widest variety of haute-cuisine dishes under one roof in Singapore. Nine areas allow you to select from Japanese, Chinese, seafood, grilled meats, or desserts from heaven. The open kitchen concept is beautifully employed, so you don't mind watching your dishes being prepared, before dining in supreme comfort. With free Moet champagne, mezza9's Sunday brunch is hard to top. 🍴 Orchard, Map p.282 B2 **51**

Halia

Newton Food Centre
Hawker Centre

Newton Circus, Newton

Quite probably Singapore's most popular hawker centre, eating late night, under the stars at Newton is still an institution. There is a labyrinth of food stalls, where you can eat fantastic local fare at low prices. Newton can be bad for touting, so avoid anyone beckoning you to their seats and agree clearly on a price before your meal is cooked, as rip-offs are not uncommon. The best thing is to sit in a seat of your choice, note your table number, place your order at a stall, tell them your table number, then pay on the arrival of the food. Arrive hungry. ◪ Newton, Map p.279 D1 🟦52

Patara Fine Thai
Thai

Tanglin Mall, Tanglin
6737 0818

Patara Fine Thai offers home-style Thai cooking as a fine dining experience. The renowned spirit of Thai hospitality and attentive service make you feel welcome as soon as you enter. Carefully selected Thai chefs, work hard to replicate the tastes you will find in Bangkok's top-end restaurants. In addition, there are fusionstyle dishes for a novel twist. Another branch is located in Swissôtel The Stamford in the Colonial District (6339 1488). ◪ Tiong Bahru, Map p.281 E3 🟦53

PS Cafe
International

28B Harding Rd, Tanglin
6479 1588

PS Cafe was undoubtedly the 'it' restaurant of 2006. With retro furniture, modern 1950s design, leafy tree views and a casual cool air, it feels more like California than Singapore. The food is fresh, inventive and good value for what you get. The staff do sometimes pack quite a lot of attitude, but PS is a refreshingly casual yet quality experience. Walk in for brunch on the weekend (unfortunately they don't take bookings) and experience the hype. 🚇 Commonwealth, Map p.280 A3 54

Samy's
Indian

25 Dempsey Rd, Tanglin   6472 2080

Understandably popular, Samy's delivers great southern Indian food served on banana leaves in a breezy open colonial building, surrounded by big shady trees. Waiters deliver delicious morsels from buckets of curry, as well as tandoori, squid, fish head curry, rice and other treats. There's no air conditioning or reservations, but cold beer is available. Sit on the verandah if you get a chance for the best views. 🚇 Commonwealth, Map p.278 C2 55

Shang Palace
Chinese

Shangri-La Hotel, Orchard   6213 4473

Traditional and ornate, Shang Palace will transport you (or attempt to, at least) to the Chinese dynasties of old. The extensive Cantonese menu is filled with exotic specialities including dim sum, seafood dishes and many imaginatively concocted options. If you are unsure what to order, the attentive staff will help you choose from a variety of tantalising signature dishes. There are set menus for couples and groups, and also a vegetarian menu. Reservations are recommended. 🚇 Orchard, Map p.281 F1 43

Song of India

33 Scotts Rd, Orchard

Indian

6836 0055

Song of India is a stately, formal and luxurious home to refined Indian haute cuisine. Set in a colonial black-and-white bungalow, nine chefs from India serve up an immense menu, drawing from all over the country, with seafood from coastal Kerala; creamy kormas and hot curries; naans and succulent meats from the tandoor; and a special emphasis on Lucknavi cuisine with its complex and delicately balanced use of spices and marinades. This restaurant sings beautifully a song of India. ⬛ Newton, Map p.282 C1 **56**

Tatsuya

Park Hotel Orchard, Orchard

Japanese

6737 1160

Acknowledged as one of the city's best sushi restaurants, Tatsuya has a loyal following. With a distinctive style of preparing its sushi, it is exceptionally tasty; and it goes without saying that the sashimi is a must try – it's firm and very fresh. Simply leave it to the chefs to orchestrate your meal, degustation style; they will create a perfect symphony of tastes that invariably leaves patrons going home incredibly happy. Reservations recommended. ⬛ Somerset, Map p.282 C3 **57**

Warung M. Nasir

69 Killiney Rd, Orchard

Indonesian

6734 6228

This humble restaurant is home to the Singaporean's dream: food which is cheap, good, and convenient – just five minutes from Orchard Road. For $5 or less, you get truly excellent Indonesian nasi padang, which consists of an assortment of spicy dishes, pre-cooked and placed in pots behind the counter. Select what you want from the choice of beef, chicken or fish curries, and it is served up with a variety of vegetables and rice. 🔲 Somerset, Map p.289 D1 **58**

Whitebait and Kale
International
1 Orchard Blvd, Orchard
6333 8025

Whitebait & Kale is a great example of Singapore's dining evolution – a restaurant that has done its homework on people's lifestyles and tastes. Without feeling too pretentious, its menu is a tasty and creative selection that mixes classic favourites with inventive food specials and new taste blends. From its open kitchen to the chalkboard specials, this is a place you could at eat every day, with smart food choices and a nicely busy atmosphere. 🔲 Orchard, Map p.281 E3 **59**

Yoshida
Japanese
10 Devonshire Rd, Orchard
6735 5014

For a thoroughly authentic Japanese sushi and sashimi bar, Yoshida is where the Japanese in Singapore go. Master sushi chef and owner Hideaki Yoshida hails from Tokyo, and has been delighting patrons for more than 20 years. The quality of the food is absolutely top-notch.and although traditional Japanese cuisine, it is exquisitely refined and designed to encourage the natural flavours of the ingredients to dance in your mouth. House specialities and mainstays include Kobe beef on hot stone, and pacific cod and sea urchin in butter sauce. Dishes are seasonal; so ask for recommendations. 🔲 Somerset, Map p.289 D1 **60**

Cafes

Bakerzin
Cafe

The Paragon, Orchard
6333 6647

Run by Daniel Tay, one of Singapore's foremost pastry chefs, this cafe is well known for its extraordinary east-west fusion food and addictive desserts. One must-try is the Otah Bruschetta; a fish paste 'cake' full of spicy ingredients wrapped in a banana leaf, barbecued, and served with ciabatta for an upper–class take on a local favourite. For dessert, try its legendary warm chocolate cake; or for a rainbow of delights, try the dessert tapas. 🚇 Orchard, Map p.282 C3 61

Cross Roads Café
Cafe

Singapore Marriott Hotel, Orchard
6831 4605

Located in the perfect place to take a break from the bustling Orchard Road, its ideal for watching the world go by over a meal or an iced tea. The menu is a mixture of local and international dishes, like steak and pasta, along with a selection of low carb, low fat and low cholesterol choices to keep health conscious diners happy. For dessert, the apple strudel and chocolate tiramisu are worth making room for. 🚇 Orchard, Map p.282 B3 62

Dôme Cafe
Cafe

9 Penang Rd, Orchard
6336 8070

Ideally located on the edge of the Orchard Road shopping belt, Dôme offers a breather from frenzied shoppers. There is a wonderful selection of periodicals available to accompany your latte, and a reasonably priced menu of items such as

Thai chicken salad or chicken mushroom pie. The spacious yet cosy ambience invites you to take it easy, mingle and enjoy good conversation: perfect for a catch-up with friends or casual business meetings. 🚇 Dhoby Ghaut, Map p.289 F1 63

Spinelli Coffee Company
The Heeren, Orchard

Cafe
6738 0233

Out of Singapore's many cafe chains, Spinelli's has some of the best coffee on the island. Among their 18 outlets, the most memorable is the ground-floor venue at The Heeren, thanks to a fantastic range of made-to-order sandwiches, salads, and fresh fruit and a large outdoor atrium, under which coffee drinkers spill out to take in the buzz of Orchard Road. Spinelli's has a consistently good range – try the ice-blended 'Original Spin' if it's hot. 🚇 Somerset, Map p.283 D4 64

Bars & Pubs

No.5 Emerald Hill Cocktail Bar
Bar

5 Emerald Hill Rd, Orchard   6732 0818

A 1910 Peranakan shophouse in the attractive Emerald Hill
area, No.5 is one of the longer-running bars in Singapore. A
sure bet for a drink any day of the week, it attracts a mix of
the after-work crowd, those looking for a relaxing chat, and
partiers starting a big night. The outdoor area has a unique
feel to it, surrounded by old shophouses and tropical foliage.
The narrow indoors has the crowded atmosphere usually
found in shophouses. 🚇 Somerset, Map p.283 D4 65

Que Pasa
Bar

7 Emerald Hill Rd, Orchard   6235 6626

Styled after a Spanish provision shop, Que Pasa is a popular
wine bar serving a wide range of wines and champagnes at
moderate prices, and an excellent selection of tapas, which
includes calamari, chorizo sausages and other authentic
Spanish treats. The bottle-lined walls, wooden tables and
chairs, and soft music create a relaxing atmosphere for a quiet
evening, while the outdoor seating amidst the attractive
historic shophouses is very pleasant in the cool of the
evening. 🚇 Somerset, Map p.283 D4 66

Ice Cold Beer
Pub

8 Emerald Hill, Orchard   6735 9929

Housed in a refurbished 1910 shophouse and next door to
Que Pasa (above), Ice Cold Beer is a popular watering hole

for cold beer at good prices, playing pool and great chicken wings, while singing to rock tunes or watching sport. That's about as fancy as Ice Cold Beer gets, and that's what makes it work. It feels like an Aussie pub, and caters to a relatively young and mixed crowd. The upstairs bar, nicknamed The Stellar Bar, is the nicest. 🗺 Somerset, Map p.283 D4 **67**

Muddy Murphy's Irish Pub   Pub
Orchard Hotel Shopping Arcade, Orchard   6735 0400

Occupying two storeys, this is Singapore's best Irish pub for atmosphere. Upstairs is a mockup of a 1900s Dublin city grocers, while downstairs plays the role of farmyard. Muddy's is especially good when it comes to live music and sport on TV. Complimented by Irish comfort food items such as beef and guinness pie and irish stew, this is a good place for a chat over a pint. 🗺 Orchard, Map p.282 A2 **68**

Nightclubs

Bar None   Nightclub
Singapore Marriott Hotel, Orchard   6735 5800

One of the most fun, live cover–band bars, Bar None is a great place for a fun night out dancing and singing along to familiar rock tracks. A good alternative to Singapore's numerous dance clubs, it fills up fast on weekends and its close proximity to the late-night Living Room bar upstairs means you can party until the wee hours. Good drinks, friendly and efficient staff and a central location make this a great place for a fun night out. 🗺 Orchard, Map p.282 B3 **62**

Sentosa

Forget about the fastfood stalls, the city's favourite getaway also has some hidden gastro gems to discover and one seriously hot beach club.

If hunger strikes you'll find all the usual suspects on Sentosa, vying to relieve your wallet of some dollars, but that money can be better spent. After a day of somewhat cheesy attractions and tourist fun, you may need a cocktail at one of the many beach bars or, Sentosa Resort & Spa (p.112) might have the perfect restaurant to make you feel like a grown-up again. Should you want to get the party started early then head to KM8 (opposite) where the drinks, beats and a Jacuzzi may mean you never want to leave.

Venue Finder

The Cliff	International	p.242
Il Lido	Italian	p.243
KM8 ⭐	Bar	p.243

Restaurants

The Cliff
The Sentosa Resort & Spa, Sentosa

International
6275 0423

With the seabreeze from the ocean nearby and eye-catching decor by Japanese designer, Yasuhiro Koichi, The Cliff is perfect for a special meal away from the city chaos. Dishes arrive at your table looking superb, and interesting creations, such as ocean trout confit with macadamia-sesame nougat, or warm chocolate truffle cake with cointreau icecream. Certainly not cheap, but an impressive spot that looks as good as its food tastes – The Cliff lives up to its reputation of excellence. ⬛ HarbourFront, Map p.299 D3 **70**

Il Lido
Italian

Sentosa Golf Club, Sentosa
6866 1977

Inspired by Venice's Lido Island, Il Lido is a modern Italian restaurant that combines hip surroundings, ocean views and a peaceful ambience. The cuisine is fantastic – soulful ingredients lovingly prepared, with staff well trained to understand food and wine. Book your table outdoors for a more romantic evening; or indoors for more buzz. For a great atmospheric meal that becomes a few cocktails and tunes later, this is a great choice. ⬛ HarbourFront, Map p.299 D3 **71**

Bars & Pubs

KM8
Bar

120 Tanjong Beach Walk, Sentosa
6274 2288

KM8 is Singapore's first beach 'day-club', and the place to party on Sentosa. Open daily (11:00 to 23:00), but busiest on the weekend (11:00 to 01:00), KM8 boasts a pool, island grooves, jugs of drinks and a sandy dance floor, and a mix of local and international DJs. The beach is the perfect excuse for a less-is-more dress code and beautiful people come out in force to heat up this trendy hangout. ⬛ HarbourFront, Map p.299 D3 **72**

Singapore River & River Valley

You'll be spoilt for choice in this waterside hub, so take a walk and decide where you fancy.

This part of town was once central to Singapore's trading industry but times have changed and it's now best known for its huge variety of restaurants and bars, not to mention some of the best clubs on the island. It is packed with eateries and with an independent brewery and the infamous Harry's, this is where you'll see the city-state's social side.

Venue Finder

Madam Butterfly	Chinese	p.249
Peony Jade	Chinese	p.249
Coriander Leaf	Far Eastern	p.246
Siam Reap II ⭐	Far Eastern	p.250
Saint Julien ⭐	French	p.249
Saint Pierre	French	p.250
Epicurious ⭐	International	p.246
Kuriya	Japanese	p.248
Café Iguana	Mexican	p.245
Cappadocia	Middle Eastern	p.245
Fish Tales	Seafood	p.246
Le Tonkin	Vietnamese	p.248
Bar Opiume	Bar	p.251
Brewerkz ⭐	Bar	p.251
Harry's Bar	Bar	p.251
Post Bar	Bar	p.252

Restaurants

Café Iguana

Mexican

30 Merchant Road, Riverside 6326 1275

With half-price house margaritas all day (except 21:00 – midnight), this is a fantastic place for dinner before heading to Clarke Quay. With more than 100 labels of tequila and mezcal, more than 11 types of margaritas, their own Iguana lager and yummy chocolate shooters, the bar is near perfect, and its solid fare is worth checking out as well. Outstanding items are the mussels, taco salad, fajitas, burritos and kahlua glazed sauteed bananas with ice cream. Reservations for dinner are essential. 🚇 Clarke Quay, Map p.289 F4 **73**

Cappadocia Café Restaurant

Middle Eastern

11 Unity St, Robertson Walk, Riverside 6732 2411

Cappadocia offers a rare opportunity to taste good Turkish and Mediterranean food; including bread, dips, shish kebabs, pizzas and vegetarian dishes. The ambience is casual and you can relax on comfortable sofas and cushions. The food offers bold, robust flavours and must-tries are the grilled prawns in lemon garlic sauce or the rolled fillet of beef stuffed with mushrooms

Going Out

Singapore River & River Valley

and spinach. There's little to wonder why this cafe/restaurant is a popular hangout. 🍴 Clarke Quay, Map p.289 E3 **74**

Coriander Leaf
Far Eastern

3A River Valley Road, Riverside   6732 3354

This restaurant scintillates the senses with its unpredictability, from the casual yet stylish mix of eastern and western influences in the decor to the Middle Eastern, Asian and Oriental cuisines prepared with western techniques. The menu features both traditional and interpreted dishes, moving from the essence of Asian cooking towards modernity, and the presentation is inspired by French traditions. Definitely worth a try, as it's so unique. 🍴 Clarke Quay, Map p.289 F4 **75**

Epicurious
International

60 Robertson Quay, Riverside   6734 7720

Fancy some gourmet comfort food while overlooking the river? Epicurious offer excellent custom-built sandwiches and other light bites at lunch while dinner features more 'grown up' bistro fare. Mismatched crockery and wooden furniture add to the charm, while outside, families, party people nursing hangovers and the occasional golden retriever, share the charming patio. Take advantage of happy hour deals or bring your own bottle ($15 corkage applies). 🍴 Clarke Quay, Map p.289 E3 **76**

Fish Tales
Seafood

Clarke Quay, Riverside   6837 3251

Fish Tales is not a typical Singaporean seafood restaurant and between the type of fish, style of cooking and

accompanying sauces, there are more than 150 ways to eat your catch. Set on the bustling strip of restaurants on Clarke Quay, the small indoor area affords an intimate and classy setting while outdoors is not the place for a romantic dinner, but the live music from restaurants next door creates a good atmosphere. 🖥 Clarke Quay, Map p.290 A4 **77**

Kuriya
Great World City, River Valley Road
Japanese
6736 0888

Kuriya deserves its reputation as one of Singapore's finest Japanese restaurants and the chefs have found the perfect marriage between classic Japanese cuisine and the innovative, contemporary flair of French cooking. Besides the extremely fresh sashimi and sushi, you can enjoy a table barbecue, claypot and grilled items. The French flair is a tour de force among the desserts: wasabi parfait with pannacotta or tofu with yoghurt and a topping similar to creme brulee. 🖥 Clarke Quay, Map p.288 B3 **78**

Le Tonkin
18 Mohamed Sultan Rd, River Valley Road
Vietnamese
6235 6006

Luxuriously plush, this fine-dining north Vietnamese and French restaurant-cum-lounge is relaxed and sophisticated with friendly service and wonderful food. Indoors, the decor includes gold-tinted hand-painted walls bathed in a warm light from the stage, while outdoors, the wicker chairs, wide sofas and a gorgeous wall of bamboo trees sequester you from the beat of the city, inviting you instead to simply unwind and enjoy. 🖥 Clarke Quay, Map p.289 E3 **79**

Madam Butterfly

Clarke Quay, Riverside

Chinese
6557 6266

With the entrance flanked by terracotta warriors and a large fishtank amid bold pinks and blues greeting you, one can tell that Madam Butterfly is a theatrical take on ancient Chinese tradition. Housed in Clarke Quay's oldest Chinese building and serving hearty, modern Chinese cuisine, this restaurant is an ideal place for big-night-out dinners, complete with colour, drama and the promise of a nightclub atmosphere downstairs. ◼ Clarke Quay, Map p.289 F4 75

Peony Jade

Clarke Quay, Riverside

Chinese
6338 0305

Situated by the Singapore River, Peony Jade simultaneously satisfies cravings for Szechuan and Cantonese cuisine. The restaurant is a converted 'godown' (dockside warehouse), now a contemporary restaurant with a touch of elegance. Try the traditional Szechuan smoked duck with camphor wood and fragrant tea leaves, or the Cantonese speciality of deep fried codfish with oat cereals. The food ranges from classics to the highly imaginative, and it draws crowds and wins awards. ◼ Clarke Quay, Map p.289 F4 75

Saint Julien

3 Fullerton Road, Riverside

French
6534 5947

With expansive views of the river and skyline, there could hardly be a more perfect venue for a fine dining restaurant than the Fullerton Water Boathouse. Awarded Restaurant of the Year for Singapore in 2006, the mood inside Saint

Julien is luxuriously sophisticated. The a la carte menu caters to a complete French fine dining experience with Brittany oysters, caviar, foie gras, shell fish, cod a la provencal, lamb, duck, pigeon, a legendary cheese platter, desserts and one of the finest wine lists of any restaurant in the city. 🚇 Raffles Place, Map p.296 C1 **82**

Saint Pierre   French
3 Magazine Road, Riverside   6438 0887

Highly creative and with an exceptionally refined interplay of flavours, the modern French dishes you find at Saint Pierre are as good as it gets in Asia. The service is warm, relaxed and highly professional and the wine matching is exceptional. For a memorable main, order the tout boeuf, 200 day aged wagyu beef served with, among other ingredients, poached foie gras, wild mushrooms, red beet braised in caramelised vinegar. 🚇 Chinatown, Map p.289 E4 **83**

Siam Reap II   Far Eastern
Asian Civilisations Museum, Riverside   6338 7596

Tucked away in one corner of the Asian Civilisations Museum, right beside the water and under a canopy of trees, Siam Reap II makes for one of the most romantic, alfresco dining experiences on the island. In the evenings enjoy the dazzling backdrop of Singapore's skyline, a live jazz band, and a spicy range of popular Cambodian, Laotian and Vietnamese dishes – all very affordable. Siam Reap II is also renowned for its hugely popular sandwiches, available for lunch. 🚇 Raffles Place, Map p.296 C1 **84**

Bars & Pubs

Bar Opiume
Bar

Asian Civilisations Museum, Riverside
6339 2876

Bar Opiume is one of the premier chill-out bars in town, and a great place to start a big night on the dance floors further down the river at Clarke Quay. From its spectacular location in the Asian Civilisations Museum, the comfortable sofas up above the riverbank offer great views of Boat Quay and the skyline of the CBD. Live jazz music keeps the atmosphere smooth and relaxed from 21:30 onwards on most nights of the week. 🚇 Raffles Place, Map p.296 C1 84

Brewerkz
Bar

30 Merchant Rd, Riverside
6438 2311

The best, and most inexpensive, in-house brewery in Singapore – Brewerkz offers great ale, free wireless broadband and delicious meals. With around eight different beers (including strawberry) and the impressive margaritas at Mexican eatery Café Iguana (p.245) next door, this is a large and well-organised operation, which manages to remain friendly. One of the best places to watch sports in Singapore, Brewerkz supports a lot of local sports teams, and bolsters many a pot-belly. 🚇 Clarke Quay, Map p.289 F4 73

Harry's Bar
Bar

28 Boat Quay, Riverside
6538 3029

Once a haunt of the infamous rogue trader Nick Leeson, Harry's Bar is the ubiquitous watering hole for bankers, traders and other workers from Singapore's financial district. A lengthy drinks menu covers every type of alcohol and more; you won't go thirsty here. There is a daily happy hour from 11:00 to 21:00, as well as a Crazy Hour (read: great deals on drinks) on weekdays from 17:00 to 19:00. There's live music seven days a week, and if you fancy a bite with your drink, Harry's offers sizeable portions of western pub food. 🚇 Clarke Quay, Map p.290 A4 87

Post Bar

The Fullerton Singapore, Chinatown

Bar
6877 8135

The place to go to celebrate or flash the cash, Post Bar in The Fullerton Hotel is so named because its ceiling was the original ceiling of Singapore's General Post Office. It now looks down on more glamourous proceedings, with uniformed bar staff, comfy couches, and an atmospheric music room. The perfect place for champagne before the opera at The Esplanade. 🚇 Raffles Place, Map p.296 C1 82

Q Bar

Empress Place, Opp Boat Quay, Riverside

Bar
6336 3386

A new addition to the scene in Singapore, Q Bar opened in 2006 offering an extensive international cocktail menu, generous house pours, generous noise on the outdoor balcony, an indoor bar and an upstairs dancefloor opening later at night. Much friendlier staff than Bar Opium next door, Q Bar is a good addition for Empress Place, and is proving – understandably – popular with a more grown-up crowd. 🚇 Raffles Place, Map p.290 B4 30

Nightclubs

Attica
Nightclub

3A River Valley Rd, River Valley Road   6333 9973

Sexy, maverick, home-grown house club Attica is popular for its use of different spaces, and attracts a good crowd. Increasingly seen as a bit of a pick-up joint, Attica has lost some of its shine, but is still a popular weekend club, and a great place to guarantee a good dance. Its outdoor garden at the back appeals to clubbers wanting a respite from the noise. 🔲 Clarke Quay, Map p.289 F4 **75**

Butter Factory
Nightclub

48 Robertson Quay, River Valley Road   6333 8243

Evidence of the popularity of R&B and hip-hop in Singapore, the main dance floor at Butter Factory gets packed every weekend, while the Art Bar plays a more edgy selection of local DJs. As they place special emphasis on promoting promising new DJ talent from across Asia, this is a great place to catch new stars in the making. A creative and friendly environment, this club is best enjoyed on the dance floor and is fun for a lively night out. 🔲 Clarke Quay, Map p.289 D3 **91**

Dbl O
Nightclub

Robertson Walk, Riverside   6735 2008

Of the clubs that attract a predominantly Singaporean audience, Dbl O (pronounced 'double oh') is among the best, with a big crowd on weekends and a mix of music styles leaning towards the commercial. This place is big, with three bars and a spacious dancefloor. Despite the reasonable cover charge and inexpensive drinks, Dbl O puts on a quality clubbing experience, making it a welcome change from the high prices found elsewhere. 🚇 Clarke Quay, Map p.289 E3 **92**

Ministry of Sound

Nightclub

Blk 3C, The Cannery, River Valley Road

6333 4168

Singapore off-shoot of the London megaclub opened in December 2005. Charging $10 to 25 entry, depending on the night and time of entry (including one drink), MOS Singapore is a 40,000 square foot venue with a main dance floor downstairs and a selection of smaller floors upstairs. Appealing to a younger audience than its rival Zouk, MOS has remained popular, and its speciality disco, house and R&B rooms have built a loyal following of their own. A good addition to the dance card in Singapore. 🚇 Clarke Quay, Map p.290 A4 **93**

Zouk

Nightclub

17 Jiak Kim Street, Riverside

6738 2988

Still Singapore's best-known club and arguably still its best, Zouk is in fact a complex of four spaces: The Wine Bar, House Club Velvet Underground, breaks room Phuture, and the three storey main space, Zouk. Thanks to an enviable international roster of visiting acts, which included stars like DJ Shadow, Sasha and Groove Armada in 2006, it has a loyal following. In fact, following the arrival of MOS, the superclub enjoyed a stunning $7 million revamp. While full entry for men to Zouk is high at $35, it covers all four spaces, and two drinks. 🚇 Clarke Quay, Map p.288 C3 **94**

Ministry of Sound

West Coast

Take the pace down a gear or two with the cafe culture and informal hangouts in this boho enclave.

Tucked between the shophouses of trendy Holland Village are some of the nicest spots for alfresco dining in Singapore, and the neighbourhood feel of the area makes for a relaxed vibe. The clusters of Lorong Mambong and Jalan Merah Saga boast some of best, including Al Hamra and Wala Wala.

Meat-eaters will be thrilled by the cuts at Brazil Churrascaria, while vegetarians and carnivores alike won't fail to be delighted by the award-winning meat-free fare at Original Sin (p.258).

A rule came into force several years ago to block the streets from cars at night so evening entertaining is even more enjoyable and popular, with patrons drinking happily under the stars when inside is too full.

Venue Finder

Colbar	International	p.257
Graze	International	p.258
Brazil Churrascaria	Latin American	p.257
Original Sin ⭐	Mediterranean	p.258
Al Hamra	Middle Eastern	p.257
Greenwood Fish Market & Bistro	Seafood	p.258
Corduroy & Finch	Cafe	p.259
Wala Wala Cafe Bar ⭐	Bar	p.259

Restaurants

Al Hamra
Middle Eastern

23 Lorong Mambong, Holland Village
6464 8488

The Lebanese food at Al Hamra is skillfully prepared and authentic, and for that extra touch, your meal is accompanied by lively Arabic music. The only modern twist on this otherwise traditional Middle Eastern fare is the concession to health-conscious customers. Enjoy your meal in air-conditioned comfort or alfresco on the sidewalk of hip, trendy Holland Village. 🚇 Buona Vista, Map p.278 B1 **95**

Brazil Churrascaria
Latin American

14 Sixth Ave, Bukit Timah
6463 1923

With 15 different cuts of meat prepared by five Brazilian chefs, this informal and lively restaurant is heaven for carnivores. You'll find an incredible selection on offer, ranging from the humble sausage and chicken to a wide variety of cuts of lamb and beef, ribs, ham and exotica such as grilled chicken hearts. Meals can be accompanied by some top wines or for a more potent punch, the caipirinha is a must-try. Reservations are strongly recommended. Map p.278 B1 **96**

Colbar
International

9A Whitchurch Rd, Queenstown
6779 4859

The Colbar is a local expatriate institution. A former canteen for British soldiers, it traces its roots back 58 years. Dishes such as ox liver with peas and chips or a chicken curry that is the toast even of noted Singapore foodies, all taste refreshingly home-cooked – not such a common quality in Singapore any longer. Its Sunday brunch is done in downscale style and worth a trip. 🖫 Commonwealth, Map p.278 B2 **97**

Graze

International
6775 9000

4 Rochester Park, Queenstown

As the name suggests, Graze is designed for dining on home-made cuisine at a leisurely pace. The restaurant is located in a black and white colonial bungalow with a romantic, alfresco dining area under the open sky. Perfect either before or after the meal is the upstairs lounge bar called Mint, with delicious cocktails, cool mellow music, and a sofa bed on the terrace, gazing over verdant gardens. 🖫 Buona Vista, Map p.278 B2 **98**

Greenwood Fish Market & Bistro

Seafood
6467 4950

34 Greenwood Ave, Bukit Timah

Fish markets hardly ever smell good, but it's worth those five seconds of breathlessness to get to this bistro behind the fresh seafood counter. Some mains particularly worth checking out are the dory with foie gras and the black cod. If you love oysters, come by on Tuesdays and indulge at $1 a pop, as long as you order a main course. And if you have space, definitely give the warm chocolate cake a go. 🖫 Commonwealth, Map p.278 C1 **99**

Original Sin

Mediterranean
6475 5605

01-62 Jalan Merah Saga, Holland Village

An award-winning vegetarian restaurant, Original Sin is hugely popular even among non-vegetarians. Flavours are so rich and tasty, you simply don't miss the meat. You have the option to dine under the stars or in the candlelit interior, surrounded by warm earthy tones. The menu respects the desires of the most stringent vegetarians; vegans and Jains can be comfortable here and the wine list is awesome. 🚇 Buona Vista, Map p.278 B2 **100**

Cafes

Corduroy & Finch
779 Bukit Timah Rd, Bukit Timah

Cafes
6762 0131

Living up to the billing of 'Deli, Cafe, Lounge', C&F is open early until late seven days a week and is a rare spot where you're guaranteed superb breakfasts and a late-night wine bar all in the same venue. Clever and decadent all at once in its menus, the restaurant is billed as comfort food and perfect for lunch, when the range is impressive, prices reasonable and sunlight floods through the windows. 🚇 Buona Vista, Map p.278 B1 **101**

Bars & Pubs

Wala Wala Cafe Bar
31 Lorong Mambong, Holland Village

Bars
6733 9400

Probably Singapore's most successful urban bar, the two-storey Wala Wala is always packed with people, spilling out onto the pavement every night of the week. Downstairs, people enjoy good pizzas and bar food with a great selection of beers. Upstairs houses more of a campus atmosphere due to the close proximity of the university, and there's a good selection of acoustic rock covers. 🚇 Buona Vista, Map p.278 C1 **95**

Culture

Singapore's short but rich history has resulted in a vibrant melting pot. Religion, ethnic origin, language and culture all combine to make this city-state truly international.

Singapore has succeeded wonderfully in creating a multicultural society with remarkable tolerance for racial and religious differences. Since the 19th and early 20th centuries, the island has been populated by immigrants, and ethnically, Singapore is inherently diverse; Chinese, Malays, Indians and Europeans have lived side by side for many generations. The race riots of the 60s spurred the government to promote a singular Singaporean identity, transcending race and religion: one is first and foremost a Singaporean, and then a Chinese, Indian, Christian or whatever. In the past 30 years, Singapore has actively solicited foreigners for employment and the city-state has become truly cosmopolitan.

Singapore has a fundamentally Chinese culture, but delve deeper and you will find a westernised and modern flavour. While 76% of residents are of Chinese origin, the primary language is English. A substantial number of Singaporeans have studied or worked in western countries, and their impact on the consciousness of the Singaporean identity has, in some form or other, diluted the Chinese influence on the culture.

Kong Meng San Phor Kark See Temple

Common traits are the importance given to family, respect for elders, and priority of communal interests over the individual's. Though culturally tolerant, Singaporeans are relatively conservative and wary of 'western liberal attitudes', in particular regarding sex and self-expression. Also characteristic of the culture is the concept of 'face', which, loosely translated, means personal dignity. Be careful not to cause someone to 'lose face' – you may not be readily forgiven.

Food & Drink

Food is an obsession with Singaporeans, and people think nothing of travelling across the island for their favourite bowl of noodles. The most popular mealtime conversation is food; people will enthusiastically exchange discoveries of a new venue or a superior version of the dish they are eating.

Singaporean cuisine (p.197) essentially refers to food from the country's predominant ethnic groups, primarily Chinese, Malay and Indian. There's also Peranakan (p.192), or nonya, food, a unique cuisine that is the result of the marriage of Chinese and Malay culture. Chinese food (p.194) can be sub-divided by dialect group; Szechuan, Cantonese and Hakka cuisine each have distinctive flair. The variety extends from fine dining (with dishes such as double-boiled shark's fin) to hawker fare at $3 a meal.

Restaurants come in all shapes and sizes and are very cosmopolitan. Quality runs from mediocre to world class and you get everything from global franchises such as McDonald's and Burger King to three star Michelin chefs whipping up magic. There also some dedicated vegetarian restaurants, including some that even serve mock meat. You can get anything from duck to a whole suckling pig, fairly close in taste and resemblance to the real thing, but made entirely of gluten. Many Hindus

Dressing Decently

Apart from nudity (read: topless for women) in a public place, which is prohibited by law, Singapore is generally tolerant towards skimpily attired men and women. It's a secular country and how much skin you show is left to personal choice. However, a certain decorum is expected in a place of worship. Women entering a mosque should cover their arms and legs, though it's not necessary to wear a head scarf. Please remove footwear before entering a Hindu or Muslim place of worship.

eat vegetarian food at least one day a week so you'll find a concentration of vegetarian restaurants in Little India (p.224). If it's food-related, Singaporeans are game to try anything, in their perennial search for something new or exotic.

Religion

No dominant religion prevails in Singapore, and the many religions co-existing mirror the country's racial diversity. Singapore is officially secular and prohibits religious teachings in public schools. The main religions are Buddhism, Islam, Christianity, Hinduism and Taoism but there's also a small number of Sikhs and Jews. Of Singapore's 10 public holidays (see p.30), six celebrate key religious events.

Christmas is the most visible religious celebration because it has been commercialised to the extent that festivities begin in early December to include Christians and non-Christians alike. Another occasion bringing the various races together is Hari Raya Puasa or Aidilfitri, celebrated at the end of Ramadan, the month-long fasting period for Muslims. Malays customarily invite friends home to feast together. Vesak Day, commemorating the birth, enlightenment and death of Buddha, is the most important day for Buddhists, who make up more than 40% of the population. It is a relatively subdued affair with devotees going to a temple in the morning to chant sutras and make offerings, followed by the ritual of releasing of captured animals such as birds, turtles and fish.

Deepavali (Diwali) or the Festival of Lights celebrates the victory of good over evil and marks the new year for

Indians. Serangoon Road, the main street through Little India, is decorated with lights, much like Orchard Road during Christmas. Families wake at 03:00 to take a traditional oil bath, and light lamps, candles and incense in their home. The opportunity to celebrate the religious event with a friend from a different faith is taken as an honour and reciprocated with great warmth and goodwill.

Politics

Singapore is a parliamentary republic based on a unitary state. There are a number of similarities to the Westminster system in the UK, one legacy from its colonial past. It has a unicameral parliament with the president as head of state. A cabinet of ministers headed by the prime minister forms the government which answers to parliament. The cabinet

collectively decides government policies. The head of state, appointed by cabinet, was a ceremonial role until 1991, when the constitution was amended to allow citizens to elect their head of state. While executive powers remain with the cabinet, the president is responsible for overseeing the use of financial reserves and has veto powers over the budget and appointments to public office. President SR Nathan, the sixth president, was re-elected in 2005 to serve a second six-year term.

General elections are held every five years. The constitution of Singapore is the supreme law and can be amended only by a two thirds majority in parliament. Provision has been made to allow the appointment of six Non-Constituency Members of Parliament and up to nine Nominated Members of Parliament with limited voting rights.

General elections are held on a 'first past the post' system and represent either single-member constituencies (electoral divisions) or group representation constituencies where political parties field several candidates. Voting is compulsory for all citizens once they reach the legal voting age of 21.

The ruling People's Action Party (PAP) has overwhelmingly dominated politics, winning all the past 10 elections. Current prime minister, Lee Hsien Loong, took office in 2004, succeeding Goh Chok Tong whose predecessor Lee Kuan Yew held office for 31 years. General elections held in May 2006 saw the PAP returned to power with 66.6% of the vote. The major opposition political parties are the Singapore Democratic Alliance led by Chiam See Tong (an alliance of several political parties), and the Workers' Party.

The Parliament

History

Singapore's strategic significance, geographically and militarily, resulted in the island being coveted by imperial powers, and becoming the economic powerhouse it is today.

The earliest record of Singapore is a third century account by the Chinese who referred to the tiny island as Puluozhong, a transliteration of Pulau Ujong, Malay for 'island at the end' of the peninsula. In the 1300s the island was known as Temasek ('sea town'), and was a focal point for trade – and a haven for pirates preying on the busy sea lanes. According to legend, Sang Nila Utama, ruler of Palembang in the 14th century, sought shelter from a storm in a tranquil fishing village on Temasek. He spotted an animal resembling a lion and renamed the island Singa Pura (lion city).

Modern Singapore was founded in 1819 when Englishman Sir Stamford Raffles of the British East India Company claimed Singapore as a regional base. After some political manoeuvrings, which included reinstating an exiled Sultan, Singapore, as part of the Straits Settlements, became a British colony. Realising the economic potential afforded by Singapore's naturally deep harbour and the convergence of trade routes at this seaport, Raffles declared the colony a free port. Consequently, Singapore flourished as traders, merchants and migrants from Malaya, Indonesia, China, India, the Middle East and Europe took advantage of its tax-free

Stamford House

status. Within 50 years of Raffles' arrival, this trading post of a few thousand had grown into a busy, cosmopolitan seaport of 85,500 people. The Chinese, mainly immigrants from southern China, became the dominant ethnic group in an ethnically diverse population.

Independence

During world war two, the British governing the colony of Singapore suffered a humiliating defeat and surrendered to the Japanese who then occupied the island from 1942 to 1945. Post-war, Singapore reverted to British rule. In 1959, Singapore achieved the constitution of a self-governing state and Lee Kuan Yew became the first prime minister after his People's Action Party won the elections. With a population of 1.5 million people, a land area of 581.5 square kilometres and devoid of natural resources, Lee believed Singapore's future lay in joining the Federation of Malaya, formed in 1963. Friction in this marriage was intense and the differences proved

Lee Kuan Yew (1923-)

Singapore's success is synonymous with former prime minister Lee Kuan Yew, and citizens view him as their founding father. He formed the socialist People's Action Party (PAP) and, at age 35, became the first prime minister of Singapore. After leading the PAP in seven victorious elections, Lee stepped down in 1990, with no loss in stature or influence. Lee still serves the Singapore government as minister mentor.

irreconcilable. On August 9, 1965, Singapore declared its independence and become the Republic of Singapore, a parliamentary democracy with a legal system based on British law.

In the 40 years since independence, Singapore's free market economy has achieved phenomenal progress and has often been cited as a model of success for emerging nations. A stable political and industrial climate, a reliable legal system, sophisticated banking and financial services, a highly educated workforce and technologically advanced infrastructure have made Singapore the favoured location for multinationals to base their headquarters and manufacturing plants in Asia. Arts and culture have also blossomed, and a fledgling film industry has emerged.

In 1990, after 31 years as prime minister, Lee Kuan Yew passed on the leadership to Goh Chok Tong. The population were housed, educated, affluent and morale was high. There was only slight concern that Singapore might falter under the second generation of leaders. Two dire events, the Asian financial crisis in 1997 and SARS in 2003, allowed the government to prove its mettle and maturity. Then in 2004, the mantle was passed on to Lee Hsien Loong, eldest son of Lee Kuan Yew.

Since 2000, the economy in Asia has experienced a major recession and its highest rate of unemployment in decades. The emergence of China and India as major economic forces in Asia is also a challenge Singapore has to step to meet. An extraordinary platform of success carries PM Lee and the third generation of leaders into a new and uncertain era.

Singapore Today

With world-class resorts, tourist facilities, entertainment and leisure – all set against a backdrop of a competitive commercial environment, the Lion City goes from strength to strength...

Singapore offers visitors a cosmopolitan destination, rich in cultural diversity and dynamic contrasts between old and new, east and west. In a single day visitors can move seamlessly from heritage-protected ethnic enclaves to ultra-modern cityscapes. Day and night, there is a phenomenal array of local and international cuisines and dining experiences. Shopping is another one of Singapore's main attractions for tourists. Singapore Tourism Board works closely with retailers to create extraordinary shopping experiences for visitors (such as the annual Great Singapore Sale p.166), where you can shop for exotic handicrafts or famous brand names at competitive prices.

Singapore is a free port and duties on items entering are only charged for cars, gasoline, tobacco and alcohol. A goods and services tax is levied on all imported items but tourists are eligible for a GST refund when they leave the country. As a result, prices of items such as electronic products, cameras, cosmetics and perfumes are very competitive compared to many other countries.

Singapore Tourism Board is spearheading plans to make the city a venue for world-class events in entertainment,

Clarke Quay

sports and the arts. After much public debate, the city will
now have two casinos in the multi-billion dollar 'integrated
resorts' located at Sentosa and Marina Bay. Singapore is also
promoting itself as a destination for natural attractions and
eco-adventure. As part of this, the southern islands, such as
Kusu, Lazarus, Seringat, the Sisters and St John's (see Outer
Islands on p.124) are being developed.

Other extensive projects are underway that will alter the
city's landscape. The Marina Bay will be transformed into a
new financial and business district, complete with residential
and commercial properties, and leisure, entertainment and
cultural facilities. Sentosa Island is being transformed into one
of Asia's top family tourist destinations and the Marina Barrage
is set to turn Marina Bay into a reservoir, providing drinking
water and a base for sporting events and activities.

Maps

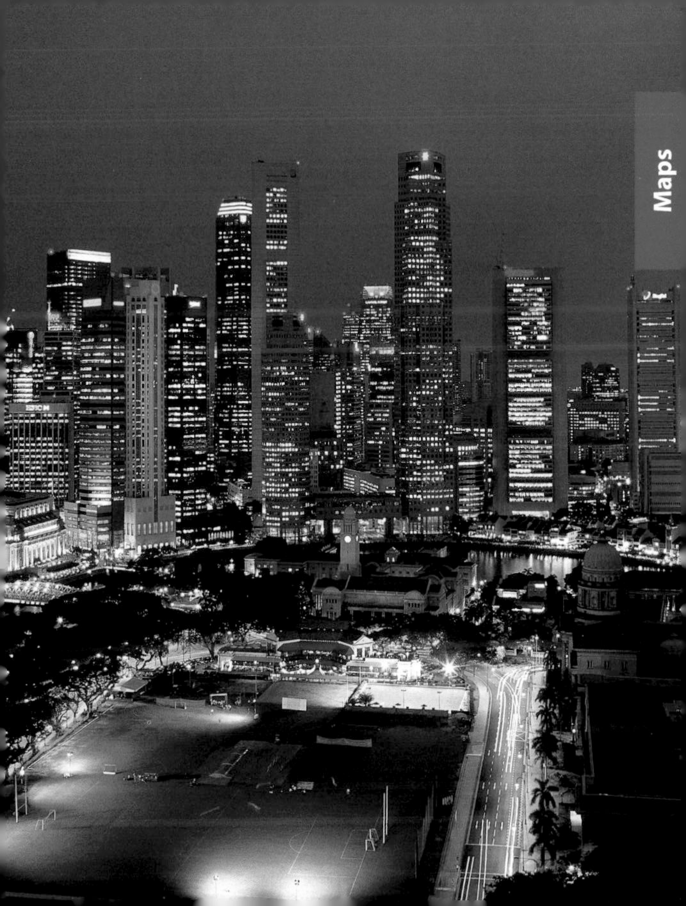

Maps

N

MALAYSIA

Causeway

Woodland Checkpoint

Woodlands

Kranji

P.300

Bukit Panjang

SINGAPORE

Choa Chu Kang

Bukit Batok

Botanic Gardens

RESTRICTED AREA

Tuas Checkpoint

Jurong

Bukit Timah

Causeway

Jurong East P.278

Clementi

Holland Village

Tanglin

Tuas

Pasir Panjang

Tiong Bahru

Queenstown

Telok Blangah

Jurong Island

Selat Jurong

Sebarok Channel

Pulau Busing

Pulau Ular

Pulau Hantu

Pulau Bukum

Selat Pandan

Pulau Bukum Kechil

Strait of Singapore

Pulau Semakau

Pulau Sakeng

Pulau Sudong

Pulau Pawai

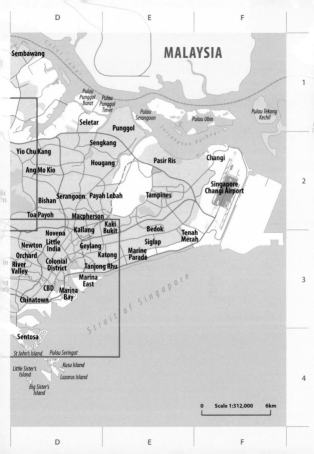

N

MALAYSIA

Sembawang

Pulau Punggol Barat
Pulau Punggol Timor
Pulau Serangoon
Pulau Ubin
Pulau Tekong Kechil

Seletar
Punggol

Yio Chu Kang
Sengkang
Hougang
Pasir Ris
Changi

Ang Mo Kio

Serangoon Harbour

Singapore Changi Airport

Bishan
Serangoon
Payah Lebah
Tampines

Toa Payoh
Macpherson

Novena
Kallang
Kaki Bukit
Bedok

Newton
Little India
Geylang
Siglap
Tenah Merah

Orchard
Colonial District
Katong
Marine Parade

River Valley

CBD
Marina Bay
Tanjong Rhu
Marina East

Chinatown

Strait of Singapore

Sentosa

St John's Island
Pulau Seringat

Little Sister's Island
Kusu Island

Big Sister's Island
Lazarus Island

0   Scale 1:312,000   6km

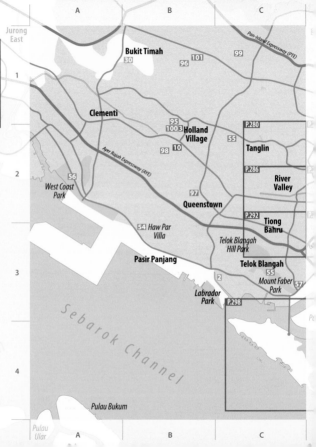

N

Jurong
East

Pan-Island Expressway (PTE)

A

B

C

Bukit Timah

30

96

101

99

1

Clementi

95
1003

Holland
Village

55

P.280

Tanglin

98

10

P.286

River
Valley

Ayer Rajah Expressway (AYE)

56

97

Queenstown

P.292

Tiong
Bahru

West Coast
Park

2

54 Haw Par
Villa

Telok Blangah
Hill Park

Pasir Panjang

Telok Blangah

55

Mount Faber
Park

57

2

3

Labrador
Park

P.298

Sebarok Channel

4

Pulau Bukum

Pulau
Ular

A

B

C

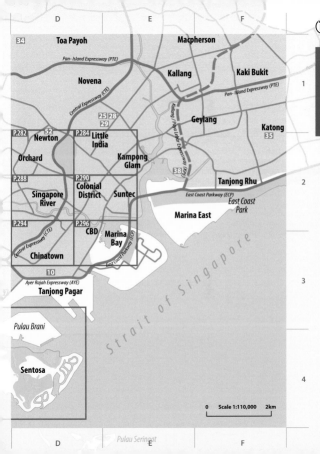

N

A   Burkill   B   Cluny Rd   C
        Hall

Tyersall Ave

Orchid
Plaza
44

Maranta Ave

1

Singapore
Botanic Gardens
41

Upper Office Gate Rd

Nassim Hill

Tyersall Ave

National
Park Board

Cluny Rd

Tamai
Gle
Ini

Swan
Lake

TANGLIN

Holland Rd

2

Main Gate Rd

Napier Rd

Youth Flying
Club

Minden Rd

Tanglin
Golf Course

Civil Service
Club

Harding Rd

Australia E

Ministry of
Foreign Affairs

54

Harding Rd

Ebenezer
Chapel

Saint George's
Church

Camp Rd

325 m

Loewen Rd

Tanglin Hill

Tanglin Rd

4

Ridley Park

Ridley Park

1000 ft

A   B   C

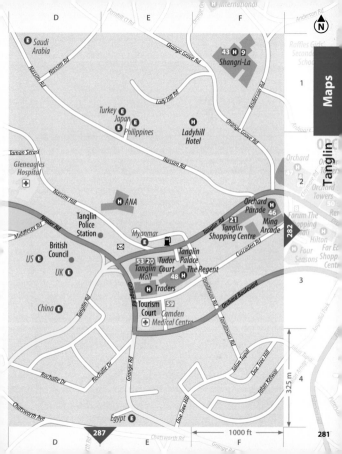

D

E

F

Anderson Rd

Saudi E
Arabia

Nassim Rd

Nassim Rd

Fernhill Ct Rd

Orange Grove Rd

43 H 9
Shangri-La

Raffles Girls'
Secondary
School

1

Lady Hill Rd

Anderson Rd

Orange Grove Rd

Ardmore

Turkey E
Japan E
Philippines E

Ladyhill
Hotel H

Orchard
Towers

Taman Serasi

Gleneagles
Hospital +

Nassim Hill

Nassim Rd

Orchard

H 47

H

2

Orchard
Towers

Napier Rd

H ANA

Tanglin
Police
Station

Middlesex Rd

Myanmar E

Orchard Rd

Tanglin Rd

21
Tanglin
Shopping Centre

Orchard
Parade H

Ming
Arcade

Cuscaden Rd

46

282

Forum The
Shopping
Mall

Hilton

Far Ea
Shopp
Cent

British
Council

US E

UK E

53 20
Tanglin
Mall

Tudor
Court

H Traders

Tanglin
Palace

48 The Regent

Tomlinson Rd

Orchard Boulevard

Four
Seasons

3

China E

Tourism
Court

59
Camden
+ Medical Centre

Rochalie Dr

Rochalie Dr

Grange Rd

Tomlinson Rd

Jalan Tupai

One Tree Hill

Jalan Kelayar

325 m

4

Chatsworth Ave

287

Egypt E

One Tree Hill

Chatsworth Rd

Grange Rd

1000 ft

281

N

Anderson Rd
Stevens Rd
national
Anderson Rd

A   B   C

Raffles Girls'
Secondary
School

Draycott Park

Stevens Rd
Stevens Rd

Goodwood Hill

Sheraton Towers
Hotel Asia **H**
56

Scotts Rd

Cairnhill Rd

Aramore Park
Draycott Dr
Draycott Dr

Hullet Rd

ORCHARD

The American
Club

Scotts Rd

39 **H**
Goodwood
Park
3

H The
Elizabeth

Orchard
47 **H**
4
68

Orchard Meritus
Towers Negara
E

Claymore Rd

13

Royal Pacific
Plaza Plaza

Far East **H**
7 Plaza

York **H**

Mount Elizabeth

Orchard Parade
H
~21
nglin
ing Centre

Orchard
Towers
50

Claymore Rd

E
Palais
Renaissance Thailand

51

H
Grand
Hyatt
Scotts
Shopping Centre

Orchard
Parade

8
Forum The
Shopping
Mall
45

Orchard Rd

Shaw
House
24

H
Hilton

Cuscaden Rd

H Four
Seasons

Far East
Shopping
Centre

Germany

E

Wheelock
Place

Netherlands,
Ireland

Marriott
62

H **10**

27 ✉
Tangs

Mount
Elizabeth
Hospital **✛**

9 **5**
7

61
14 The
4 Paragon

Bideford Rd

Park
Hotel
57 **H**

Orchard

Wisma
Atria
23

Orchard Rd

Lucky
Plaza

Angullia Park

Patterson Rd

Poland **E**

Orchard Turn

Takashimaya

26

Ngee Ann
City **12**

✉

New Zealand **E**

Orchard Boulevard

Mandarin
Gallery
H
Meritus
Mandarin

Cineleisure
Orchard

Grange Rd

ISS
International
School

Overseas
Family
School

Tanglin

Paterson Hill

Tomlinson Rd

Tengkok

Anglu

Subordinate
Courts

325 m

1000 ft

282

288

H India

Devonshire Rd

Youth
Park

Grange Rd

NEWTON

Anthony Rd

Clemenceau Ave North

Monk's Hill Rd

Winsted Rd

Hooper Rd

Bukit Timah Rd

Peck Hay Rd

Monk's Hill Secondary School

Central Expressway

Cairnhill Circle

Cairnhill Rise

Cairnhill Rd

Istana Presidential Palace

Cairnhill Circle

Cavenagh Rd

284

Emerald Hill Rd

Central Expressway

Saunders Rd

Edinburgh Rd

Sophia Rd

Mount Pa

Cornwall Rd

Sian Teck Tng Temple

Hullet Rd

Starhub Centre

38

The Heeren

64 9

65 66
67

Centrepoint Shopping Centre

Midpoint Orchard

25

Holiday Inn Park View

Cuppage Rd

Koek Rd

Cuppage Plaza

Grand Central

Cavenagh Rd

Orchard Shopping Centre

Orchard Point

Orchard Plaza

Kramat Ln

Greenore Rd

Supreme

Le Meridien

Plaza Singapura

17

UAE E

Phoenix

Orchard Rd

Buyong Rd

Methodist Centre

Cen

Somerset Rd

E Sweden

Somerset

Dhoby Ghaut

289

Exeter Rd

Eber Rd

Istana

325 m

1000 ft

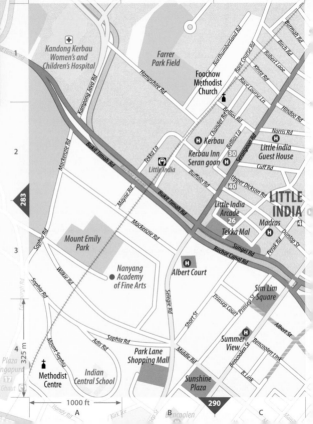

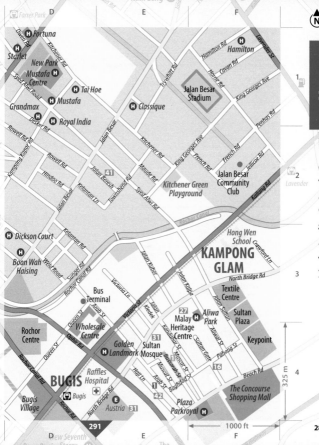

D

E

F

N

Farrer Park

Fortuna

Starlet

New Park Mustafa Centre

Tai Hoe

Mustafa

Grandmax

Royal India

Desker Rd

Jalan Besar

Classique

Hamilton

Hamilton Rd

Cavan Rd

Horne Rd

King Georges Ave

Jalan Besar Stadium

Trywhitt Rd

Kitchener Rd

King Georges Ave

French Rd

Penhas Rd

Maude Rd

Kitchener Green Playground

Jalan Besar Community Club

French Rd

Jellicoe Rd

Syed Alwi Rd

Townshend Rd

Kallang Rd

Rochor Canal Rd

Dickson Court

Boon Wah Haising

Kelantan Rd

Sungei Rd

Weld Road

Hong Wen School

Crawford St

KAMPONG GLAM

North Bridge Rd

Bus Terminal

Victoria Ln

Victoria St

Jalan Kledek

Jalan Kubor

Jalan Kubor

Jalan Sultan

Textile Centre

Sultan Plaza

Rochor Centre

Wholesale Centre

Queen St

Arab St

Capitol Rd

Golden Landmark

Sultan Mosque

Malay Heritage Centre

Aliwa Park

Aliwal St

Keypoint

Kandahar St

Muscat St

Clyde Gate

Pahang St

BUGIS

Raffles Hospital

Bugis

Bugis Village

North Bridge Rd

Rochor Rd

Austria

Haji Ln

Bali Ln

Arab St

Baghdad St

Beach Rd

The Concourse Shopping Mall

Plaza Parkroyal

1

2

Lavender

3

4

325 m

1000 ft

291

285

280

A

B

C

Ridley Park

Ridley Park

Chatsworth Rd

1

Kay Siang Rd

MINDS-Lee Kong
Chian Gardens
School

Ministry of
Education

Tanglin Rd

2

Margaret Dr

Jervois Rd

Jervois Ln

Queenstown
Secondary
School

Strathmore Rd

Clarence Ln

Crescent
Girls' School

Prince Charles Cres

Masjid
Jamae

Tanglin Rd

3

Dawson Rd

Alexandra Rd

Alexandra Rd

Viking Rd

Leng Kee Rd

Tiong Bahru Rd

4   325 m

Kung Chong Rd

Hoy Fatt Rd

Leng Kee
Community
Centre

Lengkok Bahru

Ling San
Teng Temple

Jalan Tiong

Redhill

Tiong Bahru Rd

Chang Charn Rd

TOWN

1000 ft

A

REDHILL

B

Redhill Rd

C

292

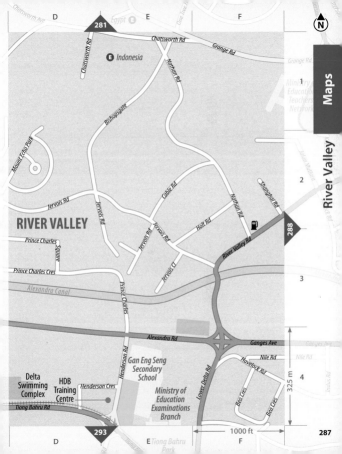

RIVER VALLEY

D E F

281

Chatsworth Ave

Chatsworth Rd

Grange Rd

Egypt

Indonesia

Nathan Rd

Bishopsgate

Chatsworth Rd

Mount Echo Park

Jervois Rd

Jervois Rd

Cable Rd

Jervois Rd

Holt Rd

Nathan Rd

Shanghai Rd

Grange Rd

Ministry of Education Teachers Network

288

River Valley Rd

Prince Charles Square

Prince Charles Cres

Jervois Cl

Jervois Rd

Prince Charles

Alexandra Canal

Alexandra Rd

Ganges Ave

Ganges Ave

Nile Rd

Nile Rd

Havelock Rd

Delta Swimming Complex

HDB Training Centre

Henderson Cres

Henderson Rd

Gan Eng Seng Secondary School

Ministry of Education Examinations Branch

Lower Delta Rd

Rasa Cres

Rasa Cres

Indus Rd

Tiong Bahru Rd

293

Tiong Bahru Park

325 m

1000 ft

287

D E F

A | B | C

282

Grange Rd

Grange Rd

E Iceland

E India

Devonshire Rd

South Park

Ministry of
Education
Teachers'
Network

Hoot Kiam Rd

Kay Poh Rd

Tivoli Bank Rd

Leonie Hill

Leonie Hill Rd

St Thomas Walk

1

River Valley Rd

Zion Murtala

Keltock Rd

Kim Seng Walk

Kim Seng Rd

River Valley
Primary School

Shanghabad

287

Zion Rd

Great World
City
78

CHIJ School

2

Zion Cl

Zion Rd

Kim Seng Promenade

Alexandra Canal

Singapore River

3

COVENT GARDEN

Park Kim St

94

Trademart
Singapore

Ganges Ave

Ganges Ave

Nile Rd

Nile Rd

Pg srupu.

Zion Rd

Ouman Rd

Grand
Copthorne

River View **H**

Havelock
Link

Havelock Rd

Havelock Rd

325 m

BUKIT HO SWEE

Zion Rd

Concorde

Copthorne
King's **H**

1000 ft

A | B | C

294

Taman Ho Swee

Novotel Apollo **H**

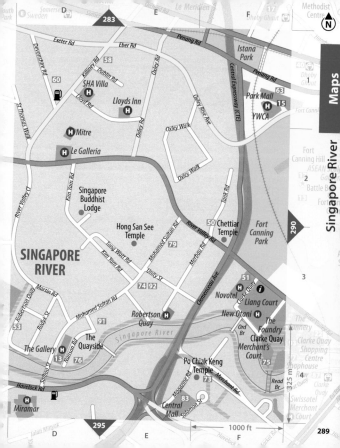

N

283

Somers Rd
Sweden
Le Méridien
Methodist Centre

Exeter Rd
Eber Rd
Penang Rd
Istana Park
17
Dhoby Ghaut
F

Devonshire Rd
Killiney Rd
Dublin Rd
Oxley Rd
Penang Rd
48
Dhoby Ghaut
1

60
58
SHA Villa
H
Lloyds Inn
H
Oxley Rise Ave
Central Expressway (CTE)
Park Mall
YWCA
H
63
15
Fort Canning

St Thomas Walk
Lloyd Rd
Oxley Walk
Fort Canning Hill
ASEAN
Garden
2
Battle Box
13
Fortgate

Mitre
H
Le Galleria
H
Oxley Walk

River Valley Rd
Kim Yam Rd
Singapore Buddhist Lodge
Tank Rd
290

Hong San See Temple
Mohamed Sultan Rd
River Valley Rd
50
Chettiar Temple
Fort Canning Park

SINGAPORE RIVER

Tong Watt Rd
Kim Yam Rd
79
Unity St
Merbau Rd
3

74
92
Clemenceau Ave
51
Clarke Quay
i
Novotel
Liang Court

Martin Rd
Robertson Quay
H
New Otani
H
The Foundry
Clarke Quay
Merchant's Court
The Cannery

Robertson Quay
Rodyk St
53
Mohamed Sultan Rd
91
Ord Br
Clarke Quay Shopping Centre
75

The Gallery
H
13
76
The Quayside
Singapore River
Swissotel Merchant Court
325 m
4

Havelock Rd
Po Chiak Keng Temple
73
Read Br

Miramar
H
Magazine Rd
Merchant Rd
Saiboo St

83
Central Mall
Solomon St

Jalan Minyak

295

0   1000 ft

289

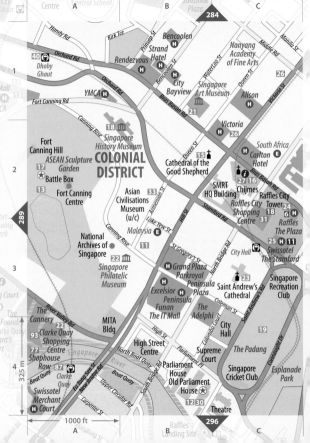

Colonial District

COLONIAL DISTRICT

N

Methodist Centre

Indian Central School

Sunshine Plaza

284

Handy Rd

Kirk Tce

Prinsep St

Bencoolen

40 Dhoby Ghaut

Orchard Rd

Rendezvous

Strand Hotel

City Bayview

Bencoolen St

Nanyang Academy of Fine Arts

Waterloo St

Middle Rd

Manila St

26

Queen St

YMCA

Orchard Rd

Fort Canning Rd

Singapore Art Museum

21

Allson

Bras Basah Rd

Victoria

Canning Rise

18 Singapore History Museum

Victoria St

26

Fort Canning Hill

ASEAN Sculpture Garden

17 Battle Box

13 Fort Canning Centre

COLONIAL DISTRICT

Queen St

15 Cathedral of the Good Shepherd

South Africa

Carlton Hotel

E

SMRT HQ Building

27 16 Chijmes

Raffles City Shopping Centre

Raffles City Tower

24

18 6

31

Raffles The Plaza

Asian Civilisations Museum (u/c)

33 Armenian St

Loke Yew St

Malaysia E

Stamford Rd

Hill St

Coleman St

National Archives of Singapore

Canning Rise

11

22 Singapore Philatelic Museum

St Gregory's St

North Bridge Rd

City Hall

25 11

Swissotel The Stamford

289

Fort Canning Park

Grand Plaza

Parkroyal

Peninsula Plaza

23 Saint Andrew's Cathedral

Singapore Recreation Club

River Valley Rd

Excelsior

Peninsula

Funan The IT Mall

The Adelphi

Coleman St

City Hall

19

The Cannery

93 Clarke Quay Shopping Centre

77 Shophouse Row

87 Clarke Quay

Liang Court

w Otani

Ord Br

The Found

Merchant's Court

MITA Bldg

High Street Centre

North Boat Quay

Singapore

River

High St

Parliament Pl

Supreme Court

Parliament House

Old Parliament House

Columbo Court

The Padang

City Hall

Singapore Cricket Club

Esplanade Park

Saint Andrew's Rd

Connaught Dr

325 m

Boat Quay

Eu Tong Sen St

New Bridge Rd

Boat Quay

South Bridge Rd

Upper Circular Rd

12 30

Theatre

Swissotel Merchant Court

Carpenter St

290

1000 ft

A

B

296

C

Raffles Landing Site

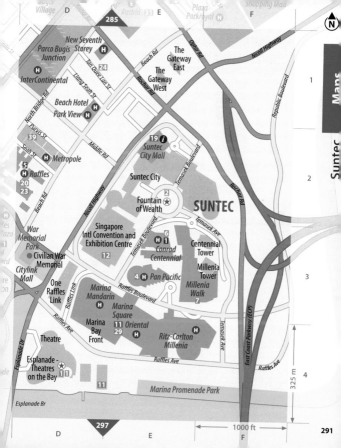

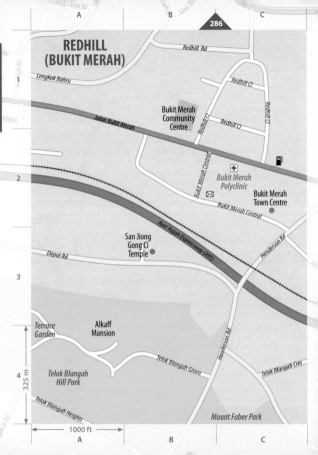

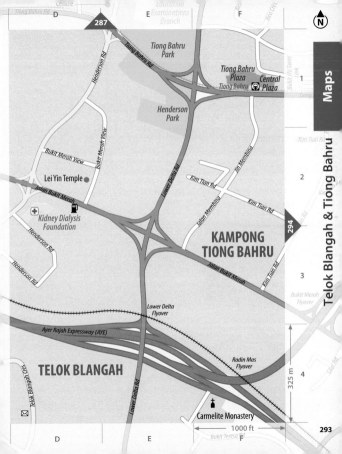

N

D
E
F

Tiong Bahru Rd

287

Education
Examinations
Branch

Bukit Ho Swee
Link

Bo Cre

Tiong Bahru
Park

Henderson Rd

Tiong Bahru Rd

Tiong Bahru
Plaza
Tiong Bahru

Central
Plaza

1

Tiong

Kim Tian Rd

Henderson
Park

Lower Delta Rd

Bukit Merah View

Bukit Merah View

Jln Membina

Kim Tian Rd

2

Lei Yin Temple

Jalan Bukit Merah

Idan Membina

Kim Tian Rd

Kidney Dialysis
Foundation

Henderson Rd

**KAMPONG
TIONG BAHRU**

3

Henderson Rd

Jalan Bukit Merah

Kim Tian Rd

Bukit Merah
Flyover

Lower Delta
Flyover

Ayer Rajah Expressway (AYE)

Radin Mas
Flyover

Sila

TELOK BLANGAH

325 m

4

Telok Blangah Cres

Radin Mas Link

Carmelite Monastery

1000 ft

D
E
F

Bukit Teresa Rd

293

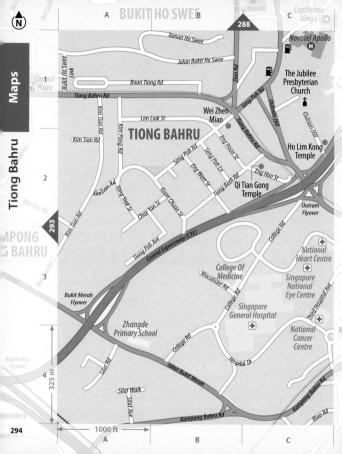

N

BUKIT HO SWEE

288

Copthorne King's

Novotel Apollo

The Jubilee Presbyterian Church

Concorde

Taman Ho Swee

Jalan Bukit Ho Swee

Bukit Ho Swee Link

Central Plaza

Boon Tiong Rd

Tiong Bahru Rd

Kim Tian Rd

Kim Tian Rd

Kim Pong Rd

Lim Liak St

Wei Zhen Miao

Seng Poh Rd

Outram Hill

Ho Lim Kong Temple

TIONG BAHRU

Eng Hoon St

Outram Hill

Seng Poh Rd

Seng Poh Ln

Eng Watt St

Tiang Bahru Rd

Eng Hoo St

Kim Tian Rd

Yong Siak St

Guan Chuan St

Chay Yan St

Tiong Poh Ave

Tiang Bahru St

Qi Tian Gong Temple

Outram Flyover

293

MPONG
G BAHRU

Xin Tian Rd

Kinta Rd

Kim Tian Rd

Tiong Poh Ave

Central Expressway (CTE)

College Of Medicine

Macalister Rd

College Rd

National Heart Centre

Singapore National Eye Centre

College Rd

Bukit Merah Flyover

Radin Mas Flyover

Zhangde Primary School

Silat Rd

College Rd

Jalan Bukit Merah

Singapore General Hospital

Hospital Dr

Third Hospital Ave

Kampong Bahru Rd

National Cancer Centre

325 m

Silat Walk

Silat Ave

onastery

Kampong Bahru Rd

Blair Rd

1000 ft

294

A | B | C

N

Map labels

83

289

296

Swissotel Merchant Court

Miramar

Central Mall

York Hill

Jalan Minyak

Outram Secondary School

Central Expressway (CTE)

Chin Swee Rd

Chin Swee Rd

Havelock Rd

New Market Rd

Hong L

Upper Pic

Subordinate Courts

Furama

Yemen

Chinatown Point

Spain

Cross St

Upper Cross St

Pearl's Hill Ter

Park Cres

Police HQ

People's Park Complex

Pearl's Hill City Park

OUTRAM PARK

Pearl's Hill Tce

Chinatown

16

Mosque St

Dragon Inn Chinatown

Backpacker Hotel

Pagoda St

Spring St

Outram Park

Pearl Bank

New Bridge Rd

Eu Tong Sen St

The Inn

Smith St

Temple St

Sri Mariamman Temple

Outram Park Shopping Complex

2

CHINATOWN

Sago St

Sago La

Outram Park

Keong Saik

Royal Peacock

Kreta Ayer Rd

Banda St

Spring St

Erskine Rd

Scarlet Boutique

Thian Hoc Keng Temp

Masjid Al-Abrar

Health Sciences Athority

National Dental Centre

Outram Rd

First Hospital Ave

Second Hospital Ave

Outram Park

Peck Lft Rd

Neil Rd

16

Kadayanallur St

3

Bus Terminal

Majestic

Bukit Pasoh Rd

Keong Saik Rd

Backpacker Cozy Corner

14

Berjaya

3

Duxton Hill

Maxwell Food Centre

Maxwell Rd

8

Telok Ayer Park

Cotgl Rd

Duxton Hill

Duxton Rd

Tanjong Pagar Rd

Tras St

Peck Seah St

Neil Rd

Park

Tanjong Pagar

325 m

Everton Rd

Everton Park

Everton Park

Cantonment Rd

Yan Kit Rd

Tanjong Pagar Community Club

Tanjong Pagar Market

Wallich St

Gopen St

Thian Guan St

Tanjong Pagar Plaza

1000 ft

(N) N

Swissotel Merchant Court

Raffles Landing Site

Asian Civilisation Museum

Empress Pl

290

The Fullerton

Fullerton Square

One Fullerton

Hongkong St

North Canal Rd

Hong Lim Park

Upper Pickering St

North Canal Rd

Upper Hokien St

Pickering St

George St

Circular Rd

Synagogue St

UOB Plaza

OCBC Centre

Chulia St

Battery Rd

Clifford Pier

China Court

Nankin St

Capital Square

Church St

Market St

Raffles Place

CBD

Ocean Building

Customs Harbour Branch

South Bridge Rd

Cross St

Mohamed Ali Ln

Club St

Telok Ayer St

Cecil St

Collyer Quay

Marina Boulevard

Backpacker Hotel

Pagoda St

295

Smith St

Sago La

Siamman Temple

Scarlet Boutique

Thian Hock Keng Temple

Masjid Al-Abrar

Hong Leong Building

Lau Pa Sat

Ann Siang Rd

Eu Tong Sen

Keong Saik Rd

Telok Ayer St

Cross St

Boon Tat St

Stanley St

Robinson Rd

Raffles Quay

East Lagoon Link

MC Callum St

Maxwell Food Centre

Maxwell Rd

Telok Ayer Park

Cecil St

Anson Rd

Maxwell Link

Boon Tat Link

Shenton Way

Shenton House

UIC Building

Singapore Conference Hall

Marina Station Rd

Tanjong Pagar

Choon Guan St

325 m

1000 ft

A B C

Esplanade Br   D   291   E   F

N

Marina Bay

MARINA BAY

Marina Bay

MARINA
BAY

5 Marina
City Park

Viewing
Hilltop

MARINA SOUTH

Marina
Bay

East Coast Parkway (ECP)

East Coast Parkway (ECP)

Marina Pl

Marina Boulevard

Marina Park

325 m

1000 ft

297

D   E   F

1

2

3

4

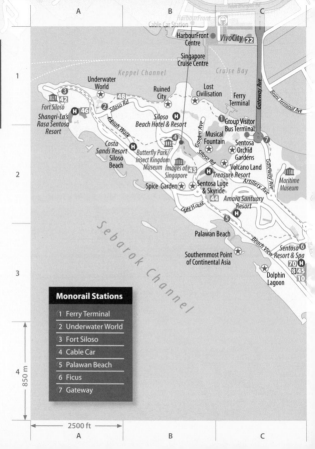

N

| A | B | C |

Telok Blangah Rd

Cable Car Station

Harbourfront

HarbourFront Centre

VivoCity **22**

Singapore Cruise Centre

Keppel Channel

Cruise Bay

1

Underwater World

Ruined City ★

Lost Civilisation ★

Ferry Terminal

Group Visitor Bus Terminal

3 🏛 42

Fort Siloso **H** 46

Shangri-La's Rasa Sentosa Resort

48

Siloso Rd

2

Rabruh Walk

Siloso Beach Hotel & Resort **H**

Musical Fountain ★

Sentosa Orchid Gardens ★

Volcano Land ★

Sentosa

7

Gateway Ave

Bukit Terminal Ave

Garden Ave

Siloso Rd

Costa Sands Resort Siloso Beach

H

Butterfly Park Insect Kingdom Museum 🏛 **4** ★

Images of Singapore 🏛

Treasure Resort **H** **53**

Artillery Ave

Maritime Museum 🏛

2

Spice Garden ★

Sentosa Luge & Skyride ★ **44**

Amara Santuary Resort

Light House

5

Palawan Beach ★

Beach View Ave

Sentosa Resort & Spa **6** **H**

70 **H**

8 **4** **5**

10

Southernmost Point of Continental Asia ★

Dolphin Lagoon ★

3

S e b a r o k   C h a n n e l

4

850 m

2500 ft

N

D E F

PULAU
BRANI

Keppel Channel

East Lagoon

Brani Terminal Ave

1

Serapong
Jetty

Serapong Course Rd

Serapong
Golf Course

Historic Site of
Sentosa Beach
Massacre Site ★

2

Serapong Hill Rd

SENTOSA

Cove Dr

Sentosa
Cove (u/c)

Bukit Manis Rd

Sentosa Cove Ave

Ocean Dr

71
E

Sentosa
Golf Club

Tanjong
Golf Course

Strait of Singapore

3

72

Tanjong
Beach

Ocean Dr

850 m

4

2500 ft

D E F

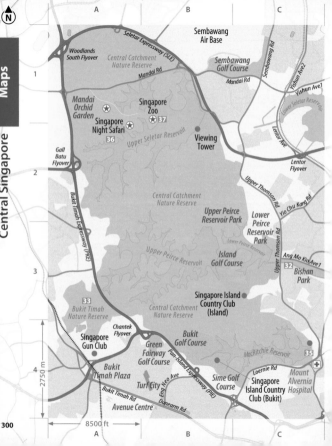

N

Sembawang
Air Base

Seletar Expressway (SLE)

Woodlands
South Flyover

Central Catchment
Nature Reserve

Mandai Rd

Sembawang
Golf Course

Sembawang Rd

Yishun Ave2

Yishun Ave1

Mandai Rd

Mandai
Orchid Garden

Singapore
Zoo 37

Singapore
Night Safari 36

Lower Seletar Reservoir

Lentor Ave

Upper Seletar Reservoir

Viewing
Tower

Lentor
Flyover

Gali
Batu
Flyover

Upper Thomson Rd

Central Catchment
Nature Reserve

Upper Peirce
Reservoir Park

Lower Peirce
Reservoir
Park

Bukit Timah Expressway (PIE)

Yio Chu Kang Rd

Upper Peirce Reservoir

Lower Peirce Reservoir

Ang Mo Kio Ave1

Island
Golf Course

Upper Thomson Rd

32

Bishan
Park

Singapore Island
Country Club
(Island)

33

Bukit Timah
Nature Reserve

Central Catchment
Nature Reserve

MacRitchie Reservoir

35

Chantek
Flyover

Bukit
Golf Course

Singapore
Gun Club

Green
Fairway
Golf Course

Pan-Island Expressway (PIE)

Loernie Rd

Bukit
Timah Plaza

Sime Golf
Course

Singapore
Island Country
Club (Bukit)

Mount
Alvernia
Hospital

Turf City

Eng Neo Ave

Bukit Timah Rd

Avenue Centre

Duneorm Rd

2750 m

8500 ft

300

Legend

These maps include what we feel are the most interesting bits of
Singapore. Shopping malls, restaurants, bars, areas to explore, activities
and spas are marked with colour coded symbols (see below).

You may also have noticed the large pull-out map at the back of the
book. This is intended to give you an overview of the city. You can detach
it from the main book, so you have even less to carry about with you. Or, if
you and a travel companion have different plans for the day, you can take
one each. So if one of you wants to shop, while the other wants to play golf,
there's no need for compromise.

23 Exploring   **23** Going Out   **23** Shopping   **23** Sports & Spas

Legend					
H Hotel/Resort		Water			Highway
🏛 Heritage/Museum		Development Area			Major Road
✚ Hospital	**CBD**	Area Name			Secondary Road
Park/Garden	**✉**	Post Office			Other Road or Track
Shopping	**★**	Place of Interest			Country Border
Education	**ℹ**	Tourist Information			Tunnel
Land	**E**	Embassy			Foot Bridge
Built up Area/Building	●	Landmark		**🚇**	MRT North South Line
Industrial Area	**†**	Church		**🚇**	MRT North East Line
Pedestrian Area	**⛽**	Petrol Station		**🚇**	MRT East West Line
					Railway
					Monorail

Index

Index

Explorer Products

Residents' Guides

All you need to know about living, working and enjoying life in these exciting destinations

Abu Dhabi

Amsterdam

Bahrain *

Barcelona *

Dubai

Dublin *

Geneva

Hong Kong

Kuwait *

London

New York

New Zealand *

Oman

Paris *

Qatar

Shanghai *

Singapore

Sydney

* Covers not final. Titles available Winter 2007.

Mini Guides

Perfect pocket-sized
visitors' guides

* Covers not
final. Titles
available
Winter 2007.

Activity Guides

Drive, trek, dive and swim… life will never be boring again

Mini Maps

Fit the city in your pocket

* Covers not final. Titles available Winter 2007.

Maps

Wherever you are, never get lost again

* Cover not final.

Photography Books

Beautiful cities caught through the lens.

Lifestyle Products & Calendars

The perfect accessories for a buzzing lifestyle

Explorer Team

Publisher
Alistair MacKenzie

Editorial
Managing Editor Claire England
Lead Editors David Quinn,
Jane Roberts, Matt Farquharson,
Sean Kearns, Tim Binks, Tom Jordan
Deputy Editors Helen Spearman,
Jake Marsico, Katie Drynan,
Richard Greig, Tracy Fitzgerald
Editorial Assistants Grace Carnay,
Ingrid Cupido, Mimi Stankova

Design
Creative Director Pete Maloney
Art Director Ieyad Charaf
Senior Designers Alex Jeffries,
Iain Young
Layout Manager Jayde Fernandes
Designers Hashim Moideen,
Rafi Pullat, Shefeeq Marakkatepurath,
Sunita Lakhiani
Cartography Manager
Zainudheen Madathil
Cartographer Noushad Madathil
Design Admin Manager
Shyrell Tamayo
Production Coordinator
Maricar Ong

IT
IT Administrator Ajay Krishnan
Senior Software Engineer
Bahrudeen Abdul
Software Engineer Roshni Ahuja

Photography
Photography Manager
Pamela Grist
Photographer Victor Romero
Image Editor Henry Hilos

Sales and Marketing
Area Sales Manager Stephen Jones
Marketing Manager Kate Fox
Retail Sales Manager
Ivan Rodrigues
Retail Sales Coordinator
Kiran Melwani
Corporate Sales Executive
Ben Merrett
Digital Content Manager
Derrick Pereira
Distribution Supervisor
Matthew Samuel
Distribution Executives
Ahmed Mainodin, Firos Khan,
Johny Mathews, Mannie Lugtu
Warehouse Assistant Mohammed
Kunjaymo, Najumudeen K.I.
Drivers Mohammed Sameer,
Shabsir Madathil

Finance and Administration
Administration Manager
Andrea Fust
Financial Manager Michael Samuel
Accounts Assistant Cherry Enriquez
Administrators Enrico Maullon,
Lennie Mangalino
Driver Rafi Jamal

Contact Us

▶ Reader Response
If you have any comments and suggestions, fill out
our online reader response form and you could win prizes.
Log on to **www.explorerpublishing.com**

▶ General Enquiries
We'd love to hear your thoughts and answer any questions
you have about this book or any other Explorer product.
Contact us at **info@explorerpublishing.com**

▶ Careers
If you fancy yourself as an Explorer, send your CV (stating the
position you're interested in) to **jobs@explorerpublishing.com**

▶ Designlab and Contract Publishing
For enquiries about Explorer's Contract Publishing arm and
design services contact **designlab@explorerpublishing.com**

▶ Maps
For cartography enquries, including orders and comments,
contact **maps@explorerpublishing.com**

▶ Corporate Sales
For bulk sales and customisation options, for this book or any
Explorer product, contact **sales@explorerpublishing.com**

Thanks to our contributing authors: Jeanne Leong, Karsten Cramer,
Luke Clark, Chia Ming Chien, Steinar Cramer, Abie Sutherland, Jean
Fung, Mark Newton, Naeema Ismail, Nik Lee and Seah Siew Hua.
Photographers: Pamela Grist, Pete Maloney and Victor Romero.

EXPLORER

Transview Golf - Suntec level

E230 - Taylormade Burner

5 wood. E260, *

Pan West Golf - Suntec level2.

Cleveland. 2 iron. R2 E115.

Nike Golf subec level 2.

* 5 wood E155.

Ngee Ann city Golf House.

Taylormade 5 wood Burner S90 180

Red American version. $401.